박문각 임용

동영상강의 www.pmg.co.kr

NEW
BuildUp
Key Terms

Guideline for Pre-service Teachers

JN412986

박현수, 유다현 공저

박문각

Preface

임용고시를 준비하는 길은 결코 쉽지 않습니다. 끝이 보이지 않는 것 같은 개념 암기, 매일 쏟아지는 새로운 자료들, 그리고 점점 쌓여가는 부담감 속에서 "내가 제대로 공부하고 있는 걸까?"라는 의문을 수없이 마주하게 됩니다. 저 역시 그 과정을 지켜보며, 임용준비생 여러분이 **길을 잃지 않고 체계적으로 공부할 수 있는 도구**가 필요하다고 느꼈습니다. 《New Build Up Key Terms》는 바로 그런 고민 속에서 출발했습니다.

저는 《New Build Up Key Terms》를 단순히 **개념을 모아놓은 요약집**으로 만들고 싶지 않았습니다. Key Term은 단순한 암기 대상이 아니라, 영어교육론을 이해하는 데 필요한 **사고의 틀**이며, 실제 시험 답안을 구성하는 데 밑바탕이 되는 **교사의 언어**입니다. 그래서 이 책은 여러분이 용어를 외우는 것을 넘어, 그것들을 **연결하여 이해하고, 시험 맥락 속에서 활용**할 수 있도록 설계되었습니다. 특히, 각 Chapter는 여러분의 학습 과정이 한 걸음씩 쌓여 나가도록 **Step 1 - 2 - 3** 구조로 구성되어 있습니다.

Step 1에서는 한 챕터의 핵심 개념들을 Semantic Map으로 제시했습니다. 큰 그림을 먼저 그려보면, 해당 영역에서 무엇을 알고 무엇을 모르는지 스스로 점검할 수 있습니다. Step 2에서는 Key Term과 Key Phrase 하나하나의 정의를 명확히 정리했습니다. 단순한 사전식 나열이 아니라, 관련된 이론과 맥락을 함께 담아 이해가 깊어지도록 구성했습니다. 마지막으로 Step 3는 이 책의 핵심인 **실제 적용 단계**입니다. Key Term은 책 속에서만 머물러서는 의미가 없습니다. 실제 임용고시에서는 이 용어들이 문제 속에 어떻게 녹아들어 출제되는지를 파악하고, 답안에서 어떻게 풀어내야 하는지를 훈련해야 합니다. Step 3에서는 Key Term이 어떤 방식으로 연결되어 나타나는지를 보여줌으로써, 여러분이 단편적인 암기를 넘어서 실전적 사고와 답안 작성 능력을 기를 수 있도록 했습니다. 이 Steps를 통해 학습하다 보면 어느새 여러분은 많고 어려웠던 Key Term에 친숙해지고 자연스러운 이해와 적용까지 완성된 지식을 얻을 수 있을 것입니다.

끝으로, 저는 이 책이 단순히 시험을 위한 요약집이 아니라, 여러분이 **교사로 성장하는 과정에서 함께할 든든한 동반자**가 되기를 바랍니다. 임용고시는 긴 여정이지만, 결국 여러분은 교실 앞에 서서 학생들을 이끌어 갈 교사가 될 사람들입니다. 이 책에서 익힌 Key Term들은 시험장에서만 쓰이고 사라지는 지식이 아니라, 여러분이 앞으로 교육 현장에서 학생들을 이해하고 지도하는 데에도 살아 움직일 것입니다.

부디 《New Build Up Key Terms》가 여러분의 불안한 마음을 조금은 가볍게 하고, 학습의 길을 선명하게 밝혀주는 **작은 등불**이 되기를 바랍니다. 지치고 힘든 순간마다, 이 책을 펼치며 다시 한번 "나는 이 길을 걸어갈 수 있다"는 확신을 얻으시길 진심으로 바랍니다.

2025년 10월
영어교육론 유다현

How to use this book

《New Build Up Key Terms》는 단순히 개념을 나열해 놓은 요약집이 아니라, 여러분이 큰 그림을 보고, 개념을 다지고, 실제 시험에 적용할 수 있도록 설계되었습니다. 각 단계를 따라가며 학습한다면, 훨씬 더 안정적이고 효율적인 학습이 될 것입니다.

1. Foundational Key Terms in ELT

먼저 Foundational Key Terms in ELT는 영어교육론을 공부하는 데 반드시 필요한 기본 개념들과 참고할 Key Term들을 모아둔 장입니다. 이후 모든 장에서 계속 반복되는 핵심 토대이므로, 본격적인 학습을 시작하기 전에 꼼꼼히 확인해 두는 것이 좋습니다. 또한 학습 도중에 헷갈리는 부분이 있을 때마다 돌아와 개념을 다시 점검하는 용도로도 활용할 수 있습니다.

◆ Activity
a reasonably unified set of student behaviors limited
some direction from the teacher, with a particular objec

◆ Approach
theoretical position about the nature of language and
and teaching

◆ Awareness
conscious attention, cognizance of linguistic, mental,
through attention and focus

◆ Awareness-raising
calling a learner's attention to linguistic factors that r
noticed

2. Map the Key Terms

각 Chapter는 Step 1. Map the Key Terms으로 시작합니다. Semantic Map은 해당 단원의 주요 개념을 한눈에 보여주는 그림이자, 여러분이 공부할 길을 안내해 주는 지도로 생각하시면 됩니다. 이 지도를 보면서 "내가 이미 알고 있는 개념은 무엇이고, 아직 부족한 부분은 무엇인지"를 표시해 보세요. 이렇게 시작하면 학습의 우선순위를 분명하게 정할 수 있고, 이후에 나올 세부 내용을 훨씬 더 잘 이해할 수 있습니다.

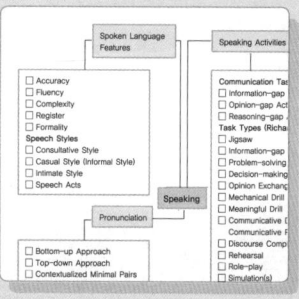

3. Master the Key Terms

다음으로 Step 2. Master the Key Terms에서는 각 Key Term과 Key Phrase의 정의를 하나씩 확인합니다. 이때 단순히 읽고 넘기지 말고, "내가 이 개념을 다른 사람에게 설명할 수 있을까?"라는 질문을 던져 보세요. 본문에는 두 가지 표시가 있습니다. 별표(★)가 붙은 항목은 중요도가 높은 개념으로, 반드시 숙지해야 합니다. 기출 표시가 붙은 항목은 실제 시험에서 출제된 적이 있는 개념이므로, 정의뿐 아니라 답안 속에서 어떻게 활용될 수 있는지도 연습하는 것이 필요합니다.

④ Global Error **
errors that hinder communication or prevent a hearer
some aspect of a message

⑤ Local Error **
errors that do not prevent a message from being
minor violation of one segment of a sentence, all
make an accurate guess about the intended meanin

⑥ Feedback Type 기출 ***
• Explicit Correction: an indication to a studen
providing a corrected form
• Recast: an implicit type of corrective feedback t
ill-formed or incomplete utterance in an unobtrus

4. Apply the Key Terms in Practice

Step 3. Apply the Key Terms in Practice에서는 앞서 익힌 개념들이 실제 문제 속에서 어떻게 활용되는지를 확인합니다. 간단한 문항을 통해 '정의 - 구별 - 적용'의 흐름을 연습하다 보면, 개념이 단순한 지식에 머무르지 않고 답안 속에서 살아 움직이게 됩니다. 중요한 것은 정답만 확인하는 것이 아니라, 무엇을 근거로 해당 Key Terms를 도출해 냈는지, 답안을 작성할 때 어떤 문장으로 풀어낼 수 있을지를 스스로 적어보는 것입니다. 반복할수록 시험장에서 개념을 자연스럽게 연결할 수 있는 힘이 길러질 것입니다.

① Audiolingualism

Read the conversation between two teachers and fill in appropriate terms.

Ms. Park : Morning! I was looking over the students' a lot of pronunciation slips.

Ms. Yoo : Yeah, I caught that too. Maybe we can kick ⓐ _____ so they can repeat the ta

Ms. Park : That should help with ⓑ _____ they'll start saying it right without even t some ⓒ _____ –like *ship* and *shee* differences better.

Ms. Yoo : Good idea. That's in line with focusing

5. Index

마지막으로, 책의 끝에 있는 Index는 복습과 마무리 학습에 큰 도움이 됩니다. 공부하다가 떠오르지 않는 용어가 있을 때, Index를 통해 해당 위치를 빠르게 찾아가 정의와 맥락을 다시 확인할 수 있습니다. 또한 스터디나 문제 풀이 중 새롭게 등장한 용어를 점검할 때도 유용합니다. 시험 직전에는 Index를 활용해 별표(*)와 기출 항목을 빠르게 훑으며 정리하면 기억의 연결고리를 강화할 수 있습니다.

이 책은 Foundational Key Terms in ELT에서 기본기를 다지고, Step 1에서 전체 그림을 그린 뒤, Step 2에서 개념을 명확히 정리하고, Step 3에서 실제 적용으로 이어지는 과정을 담고 있습니다. 마지막에 Index를 통해 복습까지 마무리한다면, 임용 준비 과정에서 흔들림 없는 든든한 학습 루틴을 만들어 갈 수 있을 것입니다.

Contents

Foundational Key Terms in ELT

✦ **Activity**
a reasonably unified set of student behaviors limited in time, preceded by some direction from the teacher, with a particular objective

✦ **Approach**
theoretical position about the nature of language and of language learning and teaching

✦ **Awareness**
conscious attention, cognizance of linguistic, mental, or emotional factors through attention and focus

✦ **Awareness-raising**
calling a learner's attention to linguistic factors that may not otherwise be noticed

✦ **Classroom-based Assessment**
instruments either created or adapted to assess classroom/course objectives

✦ **Classroom Language**
academic discourse typical of linguistic exchanges in classrooms between teacher and students and among students, often involving directions, questions, discussions, agreeing and disagreeing

✦ **Classroom Management**
the process of ensuring that classroom lessons run smoothly considering a wide range of factors from the physical arrangement of a classroom, to teaching styles and philosophy to classroom energy

✦ **Cognition**
the ability for thinking and processing information. Cognition is a general term to refer to mental activities and processes that humans engage in.

✦ **Competence**
one's underlying knowledge of a system, event, or fact; the unobservable ability to perform language, but not to be confused with performance

✦ **Comprehension**
the process of receiving language; listening and reading; input

✦ Communicative
Student responses are meaningful, real-world related, open-ended, and unpredictable.

✦ Communicative Competence (Littlewood, 2011)
- Linguistic Competence (=grammatical competence)
- Discourse Competence (=textual competence)
- Pragmatic Competence (=strategic competence): the ability to use linguistic resources to convey and interpret meanings in real situations, including those where learners encounter problems due to gaps in their knowledge
- Sociolinguistic Competence (same as Canale and Swain's definition)
- Sociocultural Competence: cultural knowledge and assumptions that affect the exchange of meanings

✦ Communities of Practice (CoP)
A group of people who share a common interest in a particular domain. Teachers of varying degrees of experience carry out their roles as practicing professionals who learn from each other. Professional development can be fulfilled not through a transmission model of education, but through a process model where teachers learn and continue to develop their skills, in dialogue with a professional community.

✦ Curriculum
a course of study that includes specifications of topics, forms, assignments, and schedules for completion; also, a group of separate courses within a program

✦ English as a Foreign Language (EFL)
generic term for English learned as a foreign language in a country or context in which English is not commonly used as a language of education, business, or government

✦ English as a Second Language (ESL)
generic term for English learned as a foreign language within culture of an English-speaking (inner circle) country

✦ English as an International Language (EIL)
English as a *lingua franca* worldwide

Foundational Key Terms in ELT

♦ Extra-class Work

assignments that a student is given to do outside the regular class hours, commonly called "homework"

♦ Extent

the rank of linguistic unit that would have to be deleted, replaced, supplied, or reordered in order to repair the sentence

♦ Eye Contact

nonverbal feature involving what one looks at and how one looks at another person in face-to-face communication

♦ Goal

the overall purpose toward which a course or a lesson is directed and is intended to achieve

♦ Group Work

a variety of techniques in which <u>two or more students</u> are assigned a task that involves collaboration and self-initiated language

♦ Kinesics

body language, gesture, eye contact, and other physical features of <u>nonverbal communication</u>. Every culture and language uses gesture or kinesics, in unique but clearly interpretable ways.

♦ Identity

the extent to which L2 learners do not perceive themselves merely as individual entities, but more importantly, as an integral and constitutive part of the social world to which they are connected

♦ Input

a term used to describe the language data that are potentially available to the learner. This includes all the visual and auditory language stimuli that surround the learner. These data could be in the form of authentically occurring language, such as an overhead conversation or written advertisement, or it could be in the form of intentionally provided examples of the language in the classroom. In other words, <u>any example of the language that the learner can potentially perceive is considered input.</u>

✦ Intake

what is actually remembered, subsumed, and internalized from various inputs to the learner, especially teacher input. It refers to the intermediary stage <u>between input and acquisition</u>.

✦ Learner Language

generic term used to describe a learner's interlanguage or interlanguage system

✦ Motivation

a psychological construct that refers to the desire and incentive that an individual has to engage in a specific activity

✦ Output

the language, either written or oral, that is produced by learners. One of the functions of output is that it helps learners to practice the L2, thereby <u>developing fluency and automaticity</u> in the target language.

✦ Pacing

the comfort level of a lesson in terms of rhythm and speed. As you are drafting step-by-step procedures, you need to look at how the lesson holds together as a whole. There are four considerations in drafting lesson plans: variety, sequencing, pacing, and timing.
- Activities are neither too long nor too short.
- Various techniques should flow together.
- Well transition from one activity to the next.

✦ Pair Work

group work in groups of two, but usually involves less complex and briefer tasks

✦ Performance

the actual production of language by a learner. Performance is sometimes distinguished from competence. The latter describes the learners' idealized abstract knowledge of the language. However, in reality, a person's linguistic performance may be less than ideal and may <u>not represent the full extent of the speaker's knowledge</u>. For example, language production may contain mistakes due to situational factors such as distraction or anxiety.

◆ Procedure

a series of actions that are performed either by a teacher or students in a certain order during the lesson

◆ Process

a progression of procedures (steps, stages, strategies, milestones) in learners' language development

◆ Product

the ultimate or end result of a set of learning efforts; for example, a final 'paper' or the summation of abilities at the end of a course of study

◆ Proficiency

a term used to refer to learners' knowledge of and ability to use the target language

◆ Rapport

(a) the relationship or connection a teacher establishes with students
(b) a relationship built on trust and respect that leads to students' feeling capable, competent, and creative

◆ Second Language Acquisition

the process of learning a language other than one's first language; the academic field of investigating how languages other than one's first language are learned

◆ Self-regulation

Sociocultural theory argues that learners go from being other-regulated, meaning that they require assistance from other people or objects in order to complete a specific task, to self-regulated, where they no longer require additional assistance.

◆ Strategy

any number of specific methods or techniques for approaching a problem or task; modes of operation for achieving a particular end; planned designs for controlling and manipulating certain information; a type of activity that learners are involved in to help them in L2 learning, L2 production or L2 comprehension

◆ Styles

consistent and enduring tendencies or preferences within an individual; general characteristics of intellectual and emotional functioning that differentiate one person from another

◆ Syllabus

a curriculum; also specifications of topics, forms, assignments, and schedules for completion of a course

◆ Technique(s)

any of a wide variety of exercises, activities, procedures, or tasks used in the language classroom for realizing lesson objectives

◆ Working Memory

a construct that refers to a temporary memory storage system used to process and rehearse linguistic input and language information retrieved from long-term memory

◆ World Englishes 기출

varieties of English spoken and written in many different countries, especially those not in the traditional inner circle (countries traditionally considered to be dominated by native speakers of English, ex. the UK, US, Australia, New Zealand) vs. outer circle (countries that use English as a common lingua franca and in which English is for many people nativized, ex. India, Singapore, the Philippines...)

Second Language Acquisition

Map the Key Terms

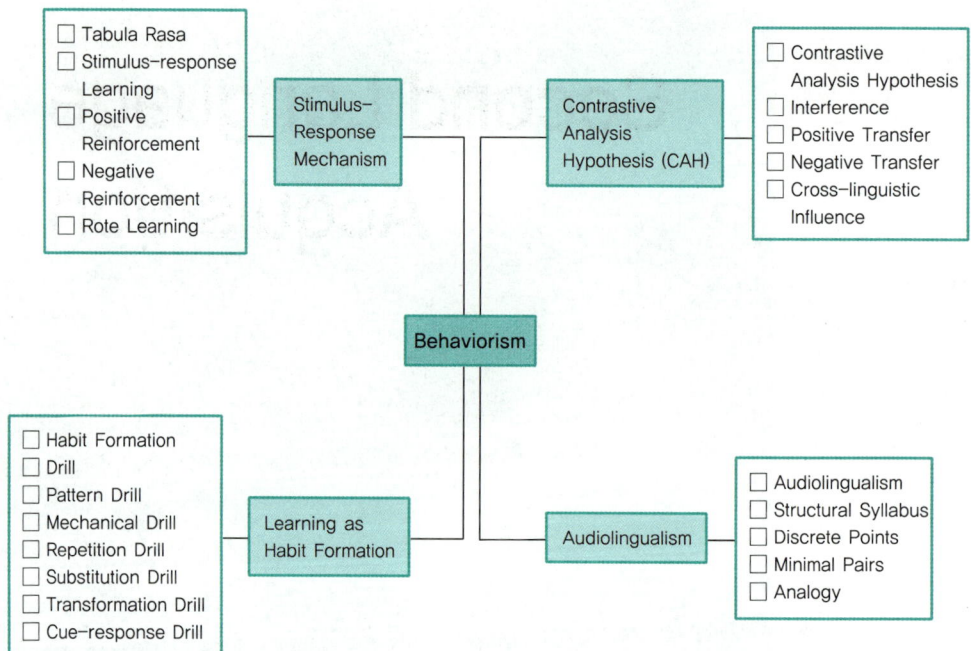

Tabula Rasa
Stimulus–response Learning
Positive Reinforcement
Negative Reinforcement
Rote Learning

Stimulus–Response Mechanism

Contrastive Analysis Hypothesis (CAH)

Contrastive Analysis Hypothesis
Interference
Positive Transfer
Negative Transfer
Cross–linguistic Influence

Behaviorism

Habit Formation
Drill
Pattern Drill
Mechanical Drill
Repetition Drill
Substitution Drill
Transformation Drill
Cue–response Drill

Learning as Habit Formation

Audiolingualism

Audiolingualism
Structural Syllabus
Discrete Points
Minimal Pairs
Analogy

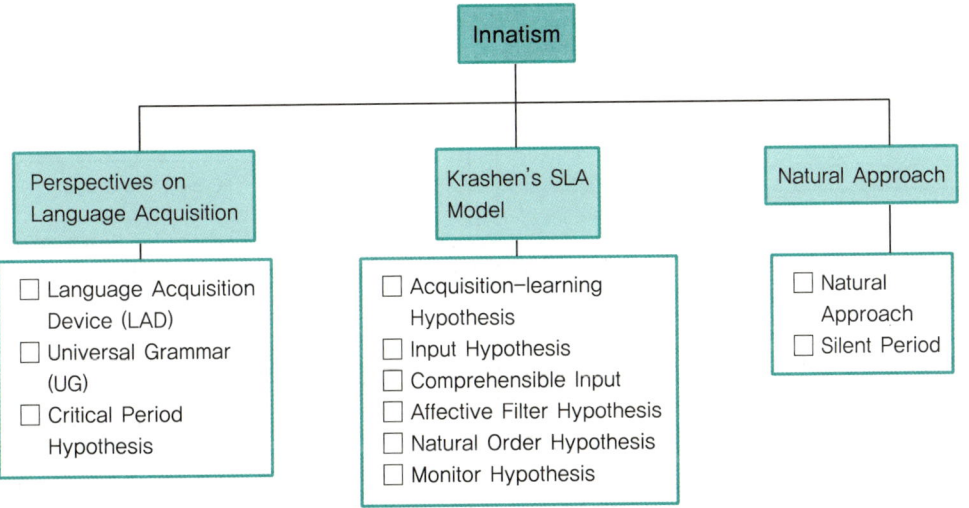

Cognitivism

Stages of Interlanguage Development
- [ ] Interlanguage
- [ ] Stabilization
- [ ] U-shaped Development/Learning
- [ ] Overgeneralization
- [ ] Backsliding
- [ ] Fossilization
- [ ] Hypercorrection

Information Processing
- [ ] Controlled Processing
- [ ] Automatic Processing
- [ ] Automaticity

Explicit-Implicit Knowledge
- [ ] Explicit Knowledge
- [ ] Implicit Knowledge
- [ ] Declarative Knowledge
- [ ] Procedural Knowledge
- [ ] Contextualized Practice
- [ ] Non-interface Position
- [ ] Interface Position

Error Analysis
- [ ] Error Analysis
- [ ] Intralingual Transfer
- [ ] Interlingual Transfer
- [ ] Global Error
- [ ] Local Error

Feedback Type
- [ ] Explicit Correction
- [ ] Recast
- [ ] Clarification Request
- [ ] Metalinguistic Feedback
- [ ] Elicitation
- [ ] Repetition
- [ ] Positive Evidence
- [ ] Negative Evidence
- [ ] Repair
- [ ] Uptake

Attention & Noticing
- [ ] Noticing Hypothesis
- [ ] Noticing
- [ ] Salience
- [ ] Noticing the Gap
- [ ] Form-focused Instruction (FFI)
- [ ] Focus on Form
- [ ] Focus on Forms
- [ ] Focus on Meaning

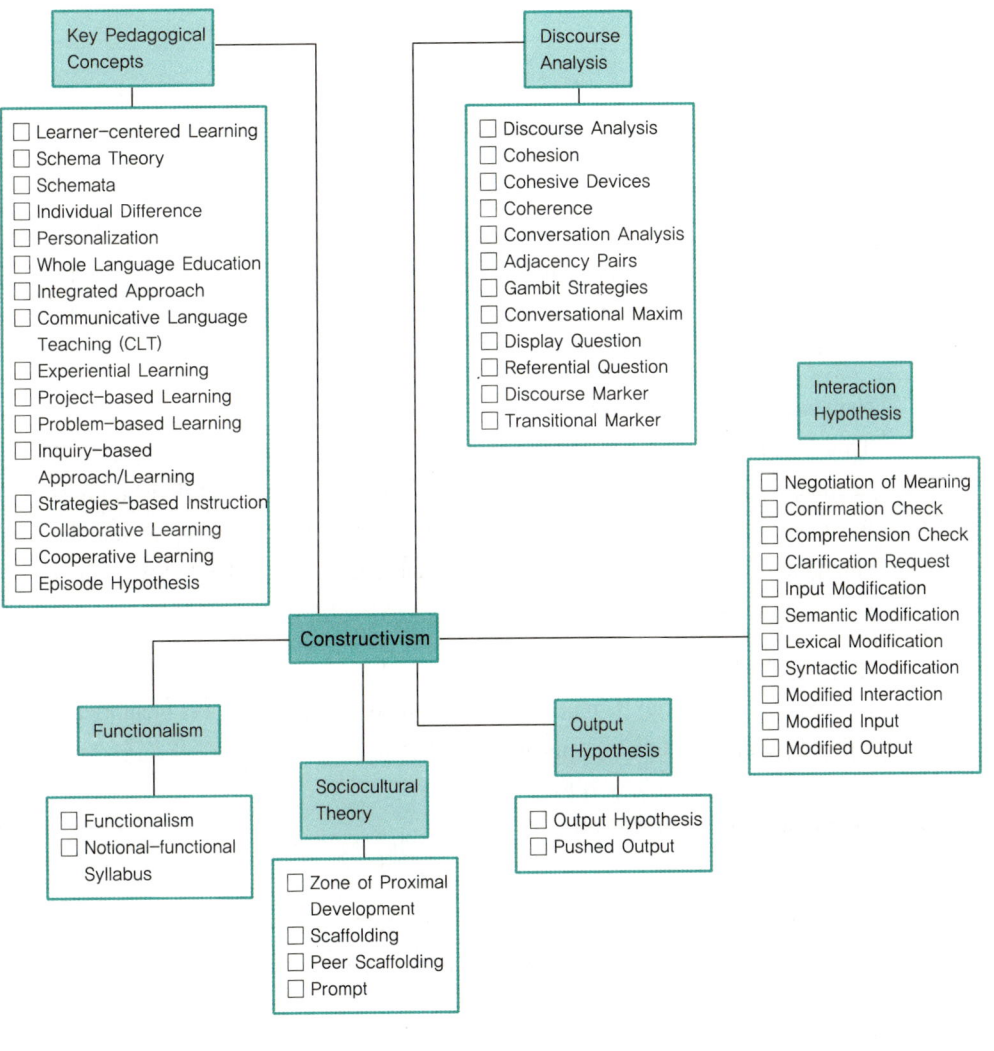

Key Pedagogical Concepts

- ☐ Learner-centered Learning
- ☐ Schema Theory
- ☐ Schemata
- ☐ Individual Difference
- ☐ Personalization
- ☐ Whole Language Education
- ☐ Integrated Approach
- ☐ Communicative Language Teaching (CLT)
- ☐ Experiential Learning
- ☐ Project-based Learning
- ☐ Problem-based Learning
- ☐ Inquiry-based Approach/Learning
- ☐ Strategies-based Instruction
- ☐ Collaborative Learning
- ☐ Cooperative Learning
- ☐ Episode Hypothesis

Discourse Analysis

- ☐ Discourse Analysis
- ☐ Cohesion
- ☐ Cohesive Devices
- ☐ Coherence
- ☐ Conversation Analysis
- ☐ Adjacency Pairs
- ☐ Gambit Strategies
- ☐ Conversational Maxim
- ☐ Display Question
- ☐ Referential Question
- ☐ Discourse Marker
- ☐ Transitional Marker

Interaction Hypothesis

- ☐ Negotiation of Meaning
- ☐ Confirmation Check
- ☐ Comprehension Check
- ☐ Clarification Request
- ☐ Input Modification
- ☐ Semantic Modification
- ☐ Lexical Modification
- ☐ Syntactic Modification
- ☐ Modified Interaction
- ☐ Modified Input
- ☐ Modified Output

Constructivism

Functionalism

- ☐ Functionalism
- ☐ Notional-functional Syllabus

Sociocultural Theory

- ☐ Zone of Proximal Development
- ☐ Scaffolding
- ☐ Peer Scaffolding
- ☐ Prompt

Output Hypothesis

- ☐ Output Hypothesis
- ☐ Pushed Output

Master the Key Terms

1 Behaviorism

(1) Stimulus-Response Mechanism

① Tabula Rasa *

blank slate

② Stimulus-response Learning *

acquiring a precise response to a discriminated stimulus

③ Positive Reinforcement *

This involves adding something pleasant or desirable to increase the likelihood of a behavior being repeated. It is a form of reward that strengthens a specific action. For example, a dog gets a treat for sitting on command, which makes the dog more likely to sit in the future.

④ Negative Reinforcement *

This involves removing something unpleasant or aversive to increase the likelihood of a behavior being repeated. It is the removal of a negative stimulus to encourage a behavior. For example, a person puts on their seatbelt to stop the annoying beeping sound in the car, which makes them more likely to wear their seatbelt in the future.

⑤ Rote Learning **

the learning of material by repeating it over and over again until it is memorized, without paying attention to its meaning

(2) Learning as Habit Formation

① Habit Formation ***

the idea that language learning is fundamentally the development of automatic, correct language habits through repeated practice and reinforcement

② Drill ***

It is a mechanical technique that focuses on a minimal number of language forms (grammatical or phonological structures) through repetition.

③ Pattern Drill ★★★

a drill that is targeted to practice some aspect of grammar or sentence formation

④ Mechanical Drill ★★

a technique with a predicted or limited set of possible responses relating to some form of reality

[ex] repetition, substitution, transformation, backward drill, cued-response drill, rejoinder

⑤ Repetition Drill ★

The teacher says models (words or phrases) and the students repeat it.

[ex] T : We bought a book.

Ss: We bought a book.

T : We bought a pencil.

Ss: We bought a pencil.

⑥ Substitution Drill ★★

a type of drill where learners practice replacing a specific word or phrase in a sentence with another, while keeping the rest of the sentence structure the same

[ex] T: We bought a book. pencil?

S: We bought a pencil.

T: eraser?

S: We bought an eraser.

⑦ Transformation Drill ★

Students are asked to transform an affirmative sentence into a negative sentence, a statement into a question, or an active sentence into a passive sentence.

[ex] T: I bought a book.

S: Did you buy a book?

⑧ Cue-response Drill 기출 ★★

giving learners a verbal or visual cue, and requiring them to produce an immediate, fixed response

[ex] picture-cued response drill

(3) Contrastive Analysis Hypothesis (CAH)

① Contrastive Analysis Hypothesis *

the claim that the principal barrier to second language acquisition is first language interference, and that a scientific analysis of the two languages in question enables the prediction of difficulties a learner will encounter. That is, it suggested that L2 acquisition involved gradual learning of the differences between the L1 and L2. The greater the differences between structures in the L1 and L2, the more difficult the acquisition of the target language was thought to be. Furthermore, structures in the L1 that were similar to structures in the L2 were more easily transferable by learners.

> • Strong Version: hypotheses or models that make broad generalizations with few (if any) exceptions, and that make claims, *a priori*, of the application of a model to multiple contexts
> • Weak Version: the belief in the possibility, *a posteriori*, that a model might apply to a specified context, once contextual variables are taken into account

② Interference 기출 ***

This term refers to the negative effects that a learners' L1 can have on learning the L2. Learners may have difficulty learning aspects of the L2 system because their knowledge of their L1 interferes with that process. Interference can be considered to be a type of negative transfer.

③ Positive Transfer *

This occurs when the learner's L1 knowledge facilitates learning the target language.

④ Negative Transfer *

This occurs when previous performance disrupts or inhibits the performance of a second task.

⑤ Cross-linguistic Influence **

a concept that replaced the contrastive analysis hypothesis, recognizing the significance of the role of the first language in learning a second, but with an emphasis on the facilitating and interfering effects both languages have on each other

(4) Audiolingualism

① Audiolingualism **

The primary focus is on speaking and listening. It viewed language learning as rote learning, repetition, and imitation. It involves learners in mechanical drills where learners repeated numerous sentences and substituted key words. Generally, it was not concerned with the semantic meaning of the sentences and not much emphasis was placed on the relevance of the sentences to the learners.

② Structural Syllabus ***

a language course that attends primarily to forms (grammar, phonology, lexicon) as organizing elements of a foreign language curriculum

③ Discrete Points ***

the teaching and testing of language through the focus on one specific item or structure at a time. Each language point is treated as a separate, isolated unit to be mastered individually.

④ Minimal Pairs 기출 ***

A minimal pair is a pair of words that differ in a single phoneme. Minimal pairs are often used to show that two sounds contrast in a language.

⑤ Analogy **

Learners form new language structures by recognizing similarities with familiar sentence patterns and applying them to new contexts, facilitating habit formation through substitution and transformation.

❷ Innatism

(1) Perspectives on Language Acquisition

① Language Acquisition Device (LAD) **

an innate, metaphorical "mechanism" in young children's brains that predisposes them to acquire language

② Universal Grammar (UG) *

a system of linguistic rules that hypothetically apply to all human languages

③ Critical Period Hypothesis *

the claim that there is a biological timetable before which and after which language acquisition, both first and second, is more successfully accomplished

(2) Krashen's SLA Model

① Acquisition-learning Hypothesis **

It states that there are two types of development. Acquisition is the development of implicit L2 knowledge that can be used to produce language in real time. Learning is the development of the knowledge about L2 rules, which can only be of limited use in helping learners to monitor their language production, but does not help in general with L2 production.

② Input Hypothesis ***

It states that input that is slightly above a learner's current interlanguage level is necessary for L2 development (i+1). Such input can be made comprehensible by the linguistic and social context. Output, in this view, does not contribute to acquisition.

③ Comprehensible Input ***

language input that contains linguistic items that are slightly beyond the learner's present linguistic competence

④ Affective Filter Hypothesis ★★★

It states that input can only become intake if learners have a low affective filter, that is to say if they view the target language and the learning context favorably. If they have high affective filter, then their resistance towards the language will interfere with their learning.

⑤ Natural Order Hypothesis ★★★

It states that the L2 develops in a specific order, similar to the development of L1 speakers of the language. Learners do not necessarily learn the structures that are most frequent in the input. Instead they acquire structures in a similar order to L1 children.

⑥ Monitor Hypothesis ★

It states that learners use their learned knowledge to monitor and, where necessary, self-correct their language production. Learned knowledge never can be the source of spontaneous speech.

(3) Natural Approach

① Natural Approach ★

a language teaching method that simulates child language acquisition by emphasizing communication, comprehensible input, kinesthetic activities, and virtually no grammatical analysis

② Silent Period ★★

This refers to the fact that children learning their first language go through a lengthy period simply listening before they venture their first words. The same phenomenon has been observed in L2 learners. It provides an opportunity to comprehend input, a prerequisite for the development of the learner's internal grammar.

③ Cognitivism

(1) Stages of Interlanguage Development

① Interlanguage **

the language system that is created by L2 learners as they develop their L2 knowledge towards the target language norms. A learner's interlanguage is systematic and rule-governed, even though the system may differ from the target language grammar. Interlanguage systems do not remain static; they are dynamic and develop as learners continue to receive input and to restructure their L2 knowledge. Instead of viewing errors as something to avoid, interlanguage theory recognizes that the 'mistakes' that learners make are to be expected as part of the learning process. (4 developmental stages: pre-systematic stage, emergent stage, systematic stage, stabilization stage)

② Stabilization *

This is a concept that refers to the fact that a learner's interlanguage system may cease develop before it achieves target-like accuracy. However, unlike fossilization, stabilization does not imply that a learner's knowledge of a specific structure cannot develop further, but rather it implies that there is no further learning at the moment. It is typically used to refer to specific linguistic structures, rather than to the learners interlanguage system as a whole. Stabilization acknowledges that as long as a learner is alive, there may be the possibilities for further L2 development.

③ U-shaped Development/Learning **

The acquisition of a linguistic structure occurs through a progression of stages, going from correct to incorrect and back to correct usage. The phenomenon of U-shaped development makes it difficult to use accuracy as a measure of language proficiency because learners may produce incorrect linguistic forms which nevertheless can represent progress towards the accurate use of the structure.

④ Overgeneralization 기출 ***

the process of generalizing a particular rule or item in the second language, irrespective of the native language, beyond conventional rules or boundaries

⑤ Backsliding 기출 ★★★

a term that refers to learners producing language that is at a lower developmental stage, even though they have progressed to a higher stage. The regression may occur because learners have not fully internalized the current developmental stage. It is a phenomenon in which the learner seems to have grasped a rule or principle and then regresses to a previous stage.

⑥ Fossilization ★★★

the relatively permanent incorporation of incorrect linguistic forms into a person's second language competence

⑦ Hypercorrection ★★★

a phenomenon in which language speakers overuse language rules in contexts where they do not apply. A speaker or writer who produces a hypercorrection generally believes (through a misunderstanding of such rules) that the form is more correct, standard, or otherwise preferable; often combined with a desire to appear formal or educated. For example, the correction of the subject-positioned "you and me" to "you and I" leads people to put it in places where they should not—such as "he gave it to you and I" when it should be "he gave it to you and me."

(2) Error Analysis

① Error Analysis ★★

the study of learner errors in the production of L2 speech and writing. Error analysis consists of the identification, description and explanation of errors. Error analysis identified two types of errors: intralingual and interlingual

② Intralingual Transfer ★

the effect of forms of one language that cannot be explained by the L1 and instead are seen as being developmental in nature. Thus, intralingual errors would presumably be made by all learners of the target language, regardless of their L1s.

③ Interlingual Transfer ★

the effect of one language on another

④ Global Error **

errors that hinder communication or prevent a hearer (or reader) from comprehending some aspect of a message

⑤ Local Error **

errors that do not prevent a message from being understood, usually due to a minor violation of one segment of a sentence, allowing the hearer (or reader) to make an accurate guess about the intended meaning

⑥ Feedback Type 기출 ***

- Explicit Correction： an indication to a student that a form is incorrect and providing a corrected form
- Recast： an implicit type of corrective feedback that reformulates or expands an ill-formed or incomplete utterance in an unobtrusive way
- Clarification Request： an interrogative utterance by which the speaker asks for explanation, confirmation or repetition of an utterance previously produced by the listener, but which has not been perfectly understood
- Metalinguistic Feedback： reponses to a learner's output that provide comments, information, or questions related to the well-formedness of the learner's utterance, without explicitly providing the correct form
- Elicitation： a corrective technique that prompts the learner to self-correct
- Repetition： in sequential reiteration of an ill-formed part of a student's utterance by a teacher

⑦ Positive Evidence **

It consists of examples of what is possible in a language. Thus, all input is potentially evidence to a learner of which linguistic structures and items can occur in the target language. There is agreement amongst all theories of SLA that positive evidence is necessary for L2 learning; however, there is controversy as to whether it is sufficient for L2 learning, with some researchers arguing that negative evidence is also necessary.

⑧ Negative Evidence **

information about what it is not possible to do linguistically in the target language. Negative evidence could come in the form of corrective feedback or explicit instruction in the target structure.

⑨ Repair ***

correction by the learner of an ill-formed utterance, either through self-initiated repair or in response to feedback

(a) (related to Conversation analysis, and Strategic competence) In the case of conversation between second language learners and native speakers, topic clarification often involves seeking or giving repair or linguistic forms that contain errors. It is part of Canale and Swain's (1983) strategic competence.

(b) (related to uptake) As a result of teacher feedback, a learner corrects an ill-formed utterance, either through self-repair or as a result of peer repair.

⑩ Uptake ***

The learner makes a response that immediately follows the teacher's feedback and that constitutes a reaction in some way to the teacher's intention to draw attention to some aspect of the student's initial utterance.

(3) Information Processing

① Controlled Processing **

Controlled processing is involved when conscious effort and attention are required to perform a task. This places demands on short-term memory. For example, a learner driver may operate a car using controlled processing, consciously thinking about many of the decisions and operations.

② Automatic Processing **

Automatic processing is involved when the learner carries out the task without awareness or attention, making more use of information in long-term memory. Many skills are considered to be 'learned' when they can be performed with automatic processing.

③ Automaticity **

being able to draw on a set of internalized procedures in order to construct spoken utterances under the pressure of time

(4) Explicit-Implicit Knowledge

① Explicit Knowledge **

information that a person knows about language, and usually, the ability to articulate that information

② Implicit Knowledge **

information that is automatically and spontaneously used in language tasks

③ Declarative Knowledge ***

consciously known and verbalizable facts, knowledge, and information

④ Procedural Knowledge ***

implicitly known knowledge that is incidentally available but not consciously verbalizable

⑤ Contextualized Practice *

practicing language in realistic, meaningful contexts, rather than in isolated drills or decontextualized exercises

⑥ Non-interface Position ***

Explicit knowledge (conscious grammar learning) and implicit knowledge (natural language acquisition) are separate systems and do not influence each other. Learning grammar rules does not lead to actual language acquisition.

⑦ Interface Position ***

Explicit knowledge can be converted into implicit knowledge through practice. Learning grammar rules helps learners notice patterns in input, leading to more effective language acquisition.

> • Strong Version: Explicit learning directly leads to acquisition. Focus on forms
> • Weak Version: Explicit knowledge helps but requires meaningful use to become internalized. Focus on form

(5) Attention & Noticing

① Noticing Hypothesis **

the hypothesis that input does not become intake for language learning unless it is noticed, that is, consciously registered

② Noticing **

- the learner's paying attention to specific linguistic features in input
- the process of the learner picking out specific features of the target language input which she or he hears or reads, and paying conscious attention to them so that they can be fed into the learning process

③ Salience 기출 ***

the degree to which a linguistic element stands out from its environment

④ Noticing the Gap ***

This concept suggests that learners need to discover the difference between their own interlanguage forms and the target language forms. One way to help learners do this is by providing them with corrective feedback when they make L2 production errors. For example, if a learner's incorrect utterance is recast by the teacher, it is hoped that the learner will notice that the reformulated correction is different from his or her own, original utterance. Another way in which learners may notice the gap in their L2 ability is in tasks such as dictogloss, in which learners are asked to reconstruct texts which they have previously heard. As learners work to recreate the text, they may realize that they do not always possess the linguistic ability that they need in order to reconstruct the text accurately.

⑤ Form-focused Instruction (FFI) 기출 ***

any planned or incidental instructional activity that is intended to induce language learners to pay attention to linguistic form

⑥ Focus on Form 기출 ***

an approach that attempts to induce learners' incidental learning by drawing their attention to target forms while they are engaged in communicative activities

⑦ Focus on Forms 기출 ***

This involves more traditional approaches to grammar that consist of isolating individual linguistic constructs out of context.

cf Focus on Meaning **

This does not allow for any attention whatsoever to the linguistic code of the L2. The assumption behind this approach is that an L2 is learned best by allowing students to experience the L2 through communication and not through rigorous study.

4 Constructivism

(1) Key Pedagogical Concepts

① Learner-centered Learning **

model of education with a focus on learners' needs and goals and individual differences in a supportive atmosphere that offers students choices and some control

② Schema Theory **

the theory that in comprehending language people activate relevant schemata, which allow them to process and interpret new experiences quickly and efficiently. Schemata serve as a reference store from which a person can retrieve relevant existing knowledge and into which new information is assimilated.

③ Schemata 기출 ***

background information that a language user brings to bear on a text

④ Individual Difference **

A wide variation in individual learning styles and personality factors is a necessary consideration in establishing the causes of success in SLA.

⑤ Personalization ***

When you personalize language, you use it to talk about your knowledge, experience and feelings.

⑥ Whole Language Education ***

an emphasis on the interconnections between oral and written language and the integration of all four skills

> • language taught as a whole, not through discrete parts
> • Language learning is experiential learning; Learner is at center and takes responsibility.
> • focus on meaning and authentic language
> • integrated skills through collaborative learning

⑦ Integrated Approach 기출 ★★★

the teaching of the language skills of reading, writing, listening, and speaking, in conjunction with each other, as when a lesson involves activities that relate listening and speaking to reading and writing

⑧ Communicative Language Teaching (CLT) ★★

an approach to language teaching methodology that emphasizes authenticity, interaction, student-centered learning, task-based activities, and communication for real-world, meaningful purposes

⑨ Experiential Learning ★★

It is an engaged learning process whereby students "learn by doing" and by reflecting on the experience. This type of learning highlights giving learners concrete experiences in which they must use language in order to fulfill the objectives of a lesson.

⑩ Project-based Learning 기출 ★★★

This is an instructional methodology in which students learn by actively engaging in real-world and personally meaningful projects. Students work on a project over an extended period of time—from a week up to a semester—that engages them in solving real-world problem or answering a complex question. They demonstrate their knowledge and skills by creating a public product or presentation for a real audience.

cf Problem-based Learning ★★★

This is a student-centered approach where learners work collaboratively to solve real-world, open-ended problems. Instead of being directly taught, students explore the problem, gather information, and propose solutions with the teaching acting as a guide.

⑪ Inquiry-based Approach/Learning ★★★

This is a student-centered approach driven by students' questions and their innate curiosity. Learners investigate the topic to find answers to the question, developing language and skills throughout the inquiry. The learner plays an active part in both their learning and the decision-making process.

⑫ Strategies-based Instruction ***

teaching learners with an emphasis on the strategic options that are available for learning; usually implying the teacher's facilitating awareness of those options in the learner and encouraging strategic action

⑬ Collaborative Learning ***

a method of teaching and learning in which students team together to explore a significant question or create a meaningful project

[ex] A group of students discusses a lecture. / Students from different schools work together over the Internet on a shared assignment.

⑭ Cooperative Learning **

an approach to teaching and learning in which classrooms are organized so that students work together in small co-operative teams. Such an approach to learning is said to increase students' learning since (a) it is less threatening for many students, (b) it increases the amount of student participation in the classroom, (c) it reduces the need for competitiveness, and (d) it reduces the teacher's dominance in the classroom.

[ex] Students work together in small groups on a structured activity. They are individually accountable for their work, and the work of the group as a whole is also assessed.

⑮ Episode Hypothesis ***

Texts which are more episodically organized can be stored and recalled more easily than less episodically organized material.

(2) Functionalism

① Functionalism *

the belief that the forms of natural languages are created, governed, constrained, acquired and used in the service of communicative functions

② Notional-functional Syllabus ***

a language course that attends primarily to functions as organizing elements of a foreign language curriculum

Chapter
01

- Notion: general (existence, space, time, quality, quantity) / specific (situations, personal identification, name, address, phone number)
- Function: identifying, reporting, denying, accepting, declining, asking permission, apologizing, requesting

(3) Discourse Analysis

① Discourse Analysis *

the examination of the relationship between forms and functions of language beyond the sentence level

② Cohesion ***

Cohesion is the grammatical and lexical linking within a text or sentence that holds a text together and gives it meaning. There are two main types of cohesion. Grammatical cohesion is based on structural content, while lexical cohesion is based on lexical content and background knowledge.

③ Cohesive Devices 기출 ***

- Grammatical Cohesive Devices: reference, substitution, ellipsis, and conjunction
- Lexical Cohesive Devices: the use of synonyms, antonyms, repetition of the same content words, words exhibiting general-specific relations(superordinate), and words displaying part-whole relations(collocation), general words

④ Coherence ***

It means the relationship among the meanings expressed in the text. Coherence names the effect of arrangements such that everything in the arrangement gives appearance of 'naturally' belonging together.

⑤ Conversation Analysis *

a type of analysis that examines talk. CA concerns with how interactional participants use language to do things and to make sense of the interaction. CA is especially interested in turn-taking and the repair of communication problems in interaction.

⑥ Adjacency Pairs ★★★

An adjacency pair is a sequence of two related utterances by two different speakers where the second utterance is a predictable/required response to the first.

⑦ Gambit Strategies ★★★

"Gambits" refer to specific conversational strategies, particularly phrases or remarks used to initiate, maintain, or navigate conversations. They act as signals to introduce topics, indicate readiness to listen, or guide the flow of the conversation.

⑧ Conversational Maxim ★★★

fundamental principles that guide effective and meaningful interactions in human communication. These maxims play a crucial role in shaping the way we convey and interpret messages in various contexts.

- Maxims of Quantity: provide as much information as in needed—no more, no less
- Maxims of Quality: do not say that you believe to be false or lack evidence for
- Maxims of Relation: be relevant to the topic of the conversation
- Maxims of Manner: avoid ambiguity and obscurity; speak clearly and orderly

⑨ Display Question ★★★

Display questions are questions asked by teachers in order that learners can 'display' their knowledge. In language classrooms, display questions are usually aimed at finding out what learners can say in the target language.

⑩ Referential Question ★★★

questions that are motivated by the need to find out something that the person asking the question doesn't know

⑪ Discourse Marker ★

Discourse markers are words or expressions that normally come at the beginning of an utterance, and function to orient the listener to what will follow. They do this either by indicating some kind of change of direction in the talk, or by appealing to the listener in some way.

cf Transitional Marker ★★

words or phrases that are used to connect sentences or pharagraphs

(4) Interaction Hypothesis

① Negotiation of Meaning 기출 ★★★

This is a process that speakers go through to reach a clear understanding of each other.

② Confirmation Check 기출 ★★★

A confirmation check is discourse move that involves a speaker verifying the meaning of a previous utterance.

③ Comprehension Check 기출 ★★★

a discourse move that involves a speaker in confirming that an interlocutor has understood the meaning of his or her previous utterance. Comprehension checks may result in the provision of modified input if the interlocutor has not understood the previous meaning.

④ Clarification Request 기출 ★★★

an utterance that tries to elicit from a speaker a revised production that is either linguistically more accurate or semantically more transparent. Clarification requests are a common type of corrective feedback because they indicate that there is a problem with the preceding utterance. Clarification requests are argued to be beneficial for learning because they require learners to produce the correct forms themselves, in contrast to other types of feedback that provide the correct form for the learner.

⑤ Input Modification ★★

Tony Lynch proposes some most common input modifications of teacher talk which are suitable especially for elementary or pre-intermediate level.

⑥ Semantic Modification ★★

paraphrasing difficult words and disambiguation

⑦ Lexical Modification 기출 ★★★

use of more common vocabulary, avoidance of idioms, use of nouns rather than pronouns

⑧ Syntactic Modification 기출 ★★★

shorter utterances, less complex utterances, more regular surface structure, increased use of present tense

⑨ Modified Interaction ★★

the various modifications that native speakers and other interlocutors create in order to render their input comprehensible to learners, similar to Krashen's comprehensible input

⑩ Modified Input ★★★

input that has been changed in some way from its original, authentic form

- Simplification: The language is made less complex by using shorter sentences, simpler grammatical forms or more commonly occurring vocabulary. There has been some suggestion that simplified talk may help with learner comprehension but that it is not helpful for longer-term development.
- Elaboration: It includes restating ideas in different ways or repeating segments of the input. Elaborated talk has been shown to have a positive effect on acquisition.

⑪ Modified Output ★★

It refers to learner's reformulation of his/her previous utterances and result in a more accurate or complex form in response to an interlocutor's corrective feedback.

(5) Output Hypothesis

① Output Hypothesis ★★

the claim, originating with Swain, that output served as important a role in second language acquisition as input because it generates highly specific input that the cognitive system needs to build up a coherent set of knowledge

② Pushed Output ★★★

the type of output that "reflects what learners can produce when they are pushed to use target language accurately and concisely"

ex When a learner is encouraged to use a correct verb tense by a teacher's provision of a recast, the learner's response to the correction can be considered pushed output.

(6) Sociocultural Theory

① Zone of Proximal Development 기출 ★★★

the metaphorical distance between a learner's existing developmental state and his or her potential development. This is "the domain of knowledge or skill where the learner is not yet capable of independent functioning, but can achieve the desired outcome given relevant scaffolded help."

② Scaffolding ★★★

the process of supporting learners' progression towards goals by providing hints, clues, reminders, examples, steps to solving a problem, encouragement, and other aids

③ Peer Scaffolding ★★

the process where learners support each other's learning by providing hints, explanations, feedback, or assistance. Through collaborative interaction, peers help each other progress toward learning goals and greater interdependence.

④ Prompt ★★

Prompts help elicit responses in the target language by giving hints or cues rather than explicit answers.

Apply the Key Terms in Practice

① Audiolingualism

Read the conversation between two teachers and fill in the each blank with the most appropriate terms.

Ms. Park : Morning! I was looking over the students' speaking work, and I noticed a lot of pronunciation slips.

Ms. Yoo : Yeah, I caught that too. Maybe we can kick off the next class with a quick ⓐ _____ so they can repeat the target pattern a few times.

Ms. Park : That should help with ⓑ _____. If they repeat it enough, they'll start saying it right without even thinking. We could throw in some ⓒ _____–like *ship* and *sheep*–so they can hear the vowel differences better.

Ms. Yoo : Good idea. That's in line with focusing on a(n) ⓓ _____ approach, where we teach one language pattern at a time.

Ms. Park : And we can use ⓔ _____–connect the new vowel sound to ones they've already learned, like *sit* and *seat*.

Ms. Yoo : Exactly. That way they'll start applying the rule to other words automatically.

② Interlanguage

Identify the five learners' error types with realistic student examples in a language classroom context.

ⓐ _____

During a speaking activity, Jiwon says :

"My father is teacher and my mother is nurse."

→ Jiwon omits the indefinite article "a" due to **negative transfer from her L1**, Korean, which does not use articles before nouns.

🔲 ⓑ _____

After learning the regular past tense rule (-ed), Minsu says:

*"Yesterday, I **goed** to the park."*

→ Minsu **over-applies the regular past tense rule to an irregular verb** ("go" → "goed" instead of "went"), because he assumes the rule applies in all cases, showing **incomplete knowledge of exceptions**.

🔲 ⓒ _____

Kyunghee, who **had been correctly using the third-person singular –s**, says:

*"My brother **live** in Busan."*

→ Kyunghee had previously said "lives" correctly but **slid back(temporary regression) to the incorrect form**.

🔲 ⓓ _____

Even though she is a **high-proficiency student**, Sanghee **repeatedly says:**

*"She **go** to school every day."*

→ Sanghee continues to omit the third-person singular –s because the incorrect form **has become permanently internalized**.

🔲 ⓔ _____

After learning that "me" is incorrect in subject position, Minjung says:

*"My friend and **I**, we did it. I mean... My friend and **I** did it–not me and my friend!"*

But later she says:

*"Between you and **I**, it was hard."*

→ Minjung tends to **over-apply a rule or correction** in an attempt to **sound more accurate or formal**.

❸ Feedback Responses to an Error

Read the conversation between the teacher and students and follow the directions.

Ms. Yoo is talking with her students about last weekend.

Ms. Yoo : So, what did you do last weekend, Jisoo?

Jisoo : I go to the beach.

Ms. Yoo : Remember, in the past tense we say I went to the beach. Can you say that?

Jisoo : I went to the beach.

Ms. Yoo : Good. And Minho, what about you?

Minho : I play soccer with my friends.

Ms. Yoo : Oh, you played soccer with your friends! That sounds exciting!

Minho : Yes, I play soccer with my friends.

Ms. Yoo : play?

Minho : Sorry! I played soccer with my friends.

Ms. Yoo : Perfect! Then, Hyejin, how about you?

Hyejin : My mom and I buyed some clothes at the department store.

Ms. Yoo : Hmm? Could you say that again?

Hyejin : My mom and I buyed some clothes.

Ms. Yoo : Your mom and you...?

Hyejin : I mean... my mom and I bought some clothes.

Ms. Yoo : Exactly, Hyejin! Jaewon, your turn.

Jaewon : I was go hiking with my family.

Ms. Yoo : Jaewon, think about the verb form after 'was'. Are we talking about an action in progress or a completed action?

Jaewon : Oh–completed. So… I went hiking with my family.

Ms. Yoo : Perfect. Now let's go back–Minho, can you tell me again what you did last weekend?

Minho : I played soccer with my friends.

Ms. Yoo : You're all perfect, guys!

Based on the classroom talk above, complete the following table with specific utterances.

Feedback Type	Teacher Feedback Utterance
Explicit Correction	ⓐ _____
Recast	ⓑ _____
Clarification Request	ⓒ _____
Metalinguistic Feedback	ⓓ _____
Elicitation	ⓔ _____
Repetition	ⓕ _____

4 Form-focused Instruction

Read the Mr. Kim's reflection on how to manage grammar instruction and fill in the blanks with appropriate terms.

> 🔲 Mr. Kim's Reflection
>
> During recent speaking activities, I noticed that several grammatical errors persisted even after repeated practice. Previously, I relied on a(n) ⓐ _____ approach, in which I pre-taught grammar structures and vocabulary in isolation. While this helped students produce correct sentences in controlled exercises, it did not always result in accurate use during spontaneous communication.
>
> To address this, I shifted to a(n) ⓑ _____ approach, drawing learners' attention to specific errors as they naturally occurred during interaction. For example, when a student said, *"He go to school every day"*, I briefly highlighted the third-person singular form in the sentence as I repeated it back: *"Yes, he goes to school every day."* This was intended to make the correct form more salient and noticeable in the input, consistent with the ⓒ _____ hypothesis.
>
> To further enhance ⓓ _____, I also used input enhancement by writing the corrected sentence on the board with the target morpheme (-s) in bold red font. This visual emphasis helped ensure that the form stood out and was more likely to be noticed.
>
> I also encouraged students to ⓔ _____ by asking students to compare their original sentence with the corrected version on the board. They underlined the part that differed and discussed why the change was necessary. This activity prompted them to consciously recognize the gap between their own output and the target form.

⑤ Current Learning Approaches

Read the conversation between two teachers and fill in the blanks with the most appropriate terms.

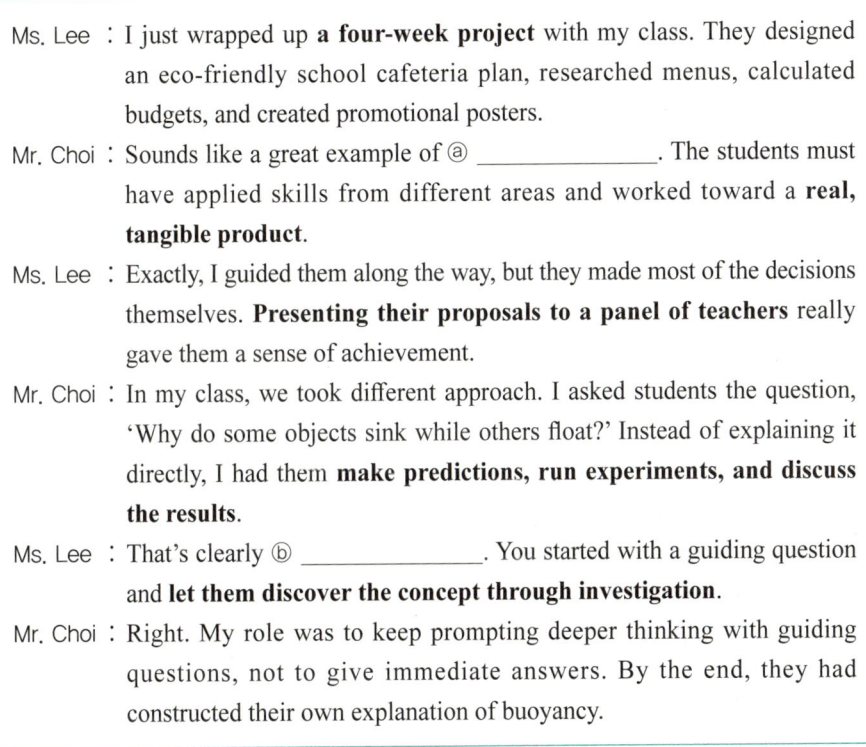

Ms. Lee : I just wrapped up **a four-week project** with my class. They designed an eco-friendly school cafeteria plan, researched menus, calculated budgets, and created promotional posters.

Mr. Choi : Sounds like a great example of ⓐ _____. The students must have applied skills from different areas and worked toward a **real, tangible product**.

Ms. Lee : Exactly, I guided them along the way, but they made most of the decisions themselves. **Presenting their proposals to a panel of teachers** really gave them a sense of achievement.

Mr. Choi : In my class, we took different approach. I asked students the question, 'Why do some objects sink while others float?' Instead of explaining it directly, I had them **make predictions, run experiments, and discuss the results**.

Ms. Lee : That's clearly ⓑ _____. You started with a guiding question and **let them discover the concept through investigation**.

Mr. Choi : Right. My role was to keep prompting deeper thinking with guiding questions, not to give immediate answers. By the end, they had constructed their own explanation of buoyancy.

6 Sociocultural Theory

Read the Ms. Park's note and follow the directions.

> 🗒 **Ms. Park's Note**
>
> During today's speaking activity, I noticed that Hana could name objects in a picture but struggled to use comparative forms correctly. I realized this was within her Zone of Proximal Development (ZPD)—a skill she could perform with guidance but not yet independently.
>
> I began scaffolding by modeling sentences such as "The library is bigger than the classroom" and providing sentence starters like "The _ _ _ _ is more _ _ _ _ than the _ _ _ _." At one point, I gave her a prompt: "How could you describe the difference between the two buildings?" This helped her focus on the target structure and encouraged her to try it herself.
>
> As she continued, her partner Jiwon offered peer scaffolding, suggesting adjectives like "taller" and "more modern," and helping her adjust the word order. I gradually reduced my own support as Hana became more confident, allowing her partner's assistance to take a greater role. By the end of the activity, Hana could produce accurate comparative sentences without any help, showing a clear progress from assisted performance to independent use—an example of successful scaffolding within the ZPD.

Based on the Ms. Park's note above, complete the table by identifying specific evidence related to the following terms.

ZPD	ⓐ _____
Scaffolding	ⓑ _____
Prompt	ⓒ _____
Peer Scaffolding	ⓓ _____

Answers

1 Audiolingualism

ⓐ drill

ⓑ habit formation

ⓒ minimal pairs

ⓓ discrete-point

ⓔ analogy

2 Interlanguage

ⓐ Interference

ⓑ Overgeneralization

ⓒ Backsliding

ⓓ Fossilization

ⓔ Hypercorrection

3 Feedback Responses to an Error

ⓐ Remember, in the past tense we say I went to the beach.

ⓑ Oh, you played soccer with your friends!

ⓒ Could you say that again?

ⓓ Are we talking about an action in progress or a completed action?

ⓔ Your mom and you...?

ⓕ play?

4 Form-focused Instruction

ⓐ focus on forms

ⓑ focus on form

ⓒ noticing

ⓓ salience

ⓔ notice the gap

5 Current Learning Approaches

ⓐ Project-based Learning

ⓑ Inquiry-based Learning

6 Sociocultural Theory

ⓐ She identifies the target skill (comparative forms) as something the learner can achieve with help.

ⓑ She models sentences and provides sentence starters.

ⓒ She asks a guiding question to elicit the target structure.

ⓓ The partner provides adjectives like "taller" and "more modern" and helps to adjust word order.

Teaching Method

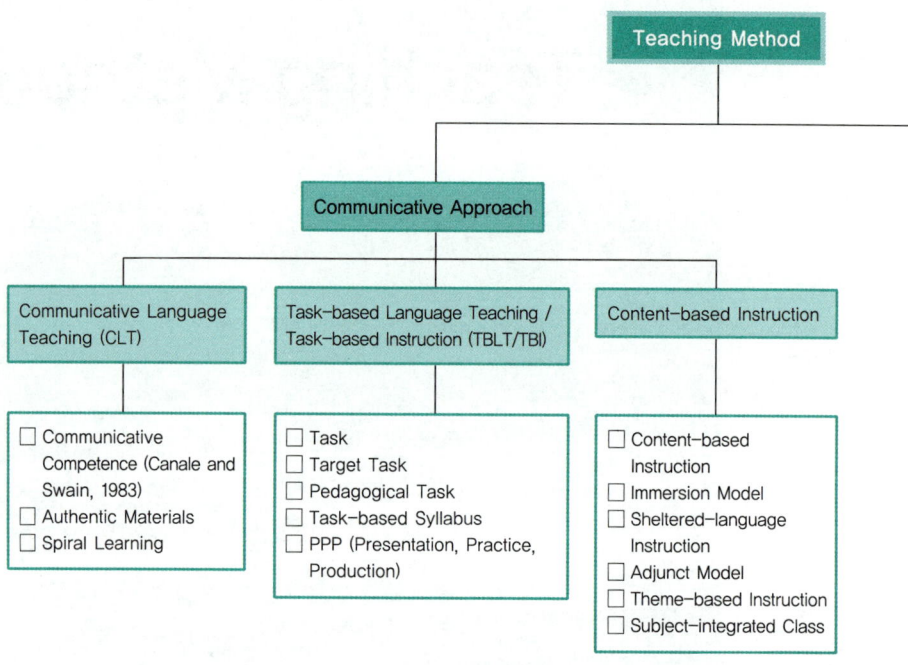

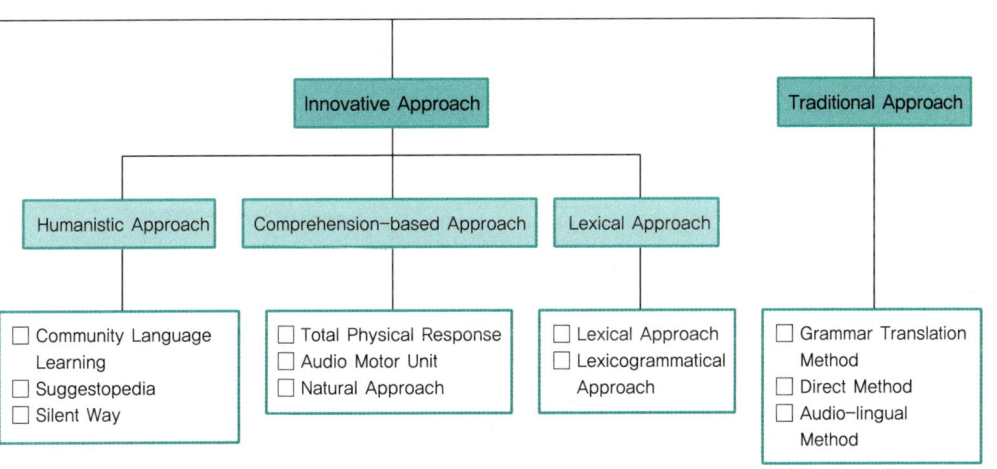

Master the Key Terms

① Communicative Approach

(1) Communicative Language Teaching (CLT)

① Communicative Competence (Canale and Swain, 1983) **

a term used to refer to a learner's ability to use language. The term, popularized in SLA, refers to learners' language knowledge that includes more than just grammatical accuracy or an idealized competence in the language. Communicative competence is seen as being composed of several different components: grammatical competence, sociolinguistic competence, discourse competence, strategic competence.

- Grammatical Competence *: knowledge of lexical items and of rules of morphology, syntax, sentence-grammar semantics, and phonology. It is the competence we associate with mastering the linguistic code of a language, the linguistic competence referred to by Hymes (1972) and Paulston (1974).
- Sociolinguistic Competence **: the ability to follow sociocultural rules of language. This requires an understanding of the social context in which language is used: the roles of the participants, the information they share, and the function of the interaction.
- Discourse Competence **: the ability to connect sentences in stretches of discourse and to form a meaningful whole out of a series of utterances. With its inter-sentential relationships, discourse encompasses everything from simple spoken conversations to lengthy written texts (articles, books, etc).
- Strategic Competence **: the ability to use verbal and nonverbal communicative techniques to compensate for breakdowns in communication or insufficient competence. It includes the ability to make "repairs" and to sustain communication through paraphrase, circumlocution, repetition, avoidance, and guessing.

② Authentic Materials ***

materials that are originally created for real-life communication outside the classroom, not specifically for teaching purposes. They reflect natural language as it is actually used by native speakers.

③ Spiral Learning ★★★

(a) a teaching method based on the premise that a learner learns more about a subject each time the topic is reviewed or encountered. The idea is that each time a learner encounters the topic, the student expands their knowledge or improves their skill level.

(b) a technique often used in education where the initial focus of instruction is the basic facts of a subject, with further details being introduced as learning progresses. Throughout instruction, both the initial basic facts and the relationships to later details are repeatedly emphasized to help enter into long-term memory.

⬦ Key principles of a spiral curriculum

- Topics are revisited.
- Levels of difficulty increase.
- New learning is related to previous learning.

(2) Task-based Language Teaching / Task-based Instruction (TBLT/TBI)

① Task ★★

a classroom activity in which meaning is primary, there is a problem to solve, a relationship to real-world activities, and an objective that can be assessed in terms of an outcome

② Target Task ★★

It uses language in the world beyond the classroom that becomes the focus of classroom instruction.

③ Pedagogical Task ★★★

any of a sequence of techniques designed ultimately to teach students to perform the target task

④ Task-based Syllabus 기출 ★★★

This does not organize the teaching with the linguistic features of the language being learned. It contains a series of complex and purposeful tasks that the students want or need to perform with the language they are learning.

⑤ PPP (Presentation, Practice, Production) ★★★

This is a method of language instruction that involves the explicit presentation of specific linguistic forms, such as vocabulary items or grammar rules. This presentation is followed by controlled learner practice of the target forms. Finally, freer production in using the forms is allowed. PPP is often associated with more traditional types of L2 instruction, in which the target language is presented in a largely decontextualized, non-communicative context. It does not allow learners to use the language items for primarily communicative purposes.

(3) Content-based Instruction

① Content-based Instruction ★★★

an umbrella term for multifaceted approach to second or foreign language teaching that shares a common point of departure—the integration of language teaching aims with content instruction. This is a programme in English as a second language in which the focus is on teaching students the skills they will need in regular classrooms(〔ex〕 for learning in the content area such as maths, geography, or biology). Such a programme teaches students the language skills they will need when they are mainstreamed.

② Immersion Model ★★★

a type of education that involves placing L2 learners in an environment primarily comprised of the target language. Learners study academic content, such as math, science, and history in the target language.

③ Sheltered-language Instruction ★★

This involves the deliberate separation of L2 students from native speakers of the target language for the purpose of content instruction. For L2 students whose language proficiency is not quite able to handle subject-matter content in the L1 of the educational system, they provide opportunities for them to master content standards with added language assistance. In such cases, the teach of a school subject (science, history) modifies the presentation of material to help L2 learners process the content. Pre-teaching difficult vocabulary, suggesting reading comprehension strategies, explaining certain grammatical structures, and offering, form-focused feedback are among techniques that have shown to be helpful.

④ **Adjunct Model** ★★★

linking subject-matter teachers and language teachers in content-based courses

⑤ **Theme-based Instruction** ★★★

When language courses are organized around meaningful situations or topics, they may be said to be theme-based, sometimes referred to as topic-based curricula. Theme-based instruction can serve multiple interests of students in a classroom and can offer a focus on content while still adhering to institutional requirements for coverage of grammatical criteria.

cf **Subject-integrated Class** ★★★

교과 간 통합수업은 내용중심 교육의 약화된 모델로, 내용과 언어 모두를 가르치는 데 초점을 두고 있다. 주제중심의 교육은 학생들의 흥미를 고려하여 주제를 선정하고 이와 관련된 활동을 바탕으로 영어를 지도하는 방법이다. 따라서 다양한 주제를 중심으로 이와 관련된 타 교과 과목과 통합하여 영어를 지도할 수 있다. Brown(2001)은 전통적인 언어 수업에 대한 대안으로 주제나 소재를 중심으로 수업을 수행할 경우 자동화, 유의적인 학습, 내적 동기 및 의사소통 능력과 관련된 원리에 입각하여 실용적이고 효과적으로 언어를 가르칠 수 있다고 언급하고 있다. 즉, 다른 교과의 소재를 활용하여 영어 수업을 진행하기 때문에 그 교과의 내용을 예습 혹은 복습하는 효과를 얻을 수 있을 뿐만 아니라 영어로 다양한 분야의 내용을 배울 수 있다는 효과가 있다. 따라서 이 교육방법에서는 수업시간에 다루게 될 주제나 소재의 선별이 매우 중요하다.

② Innovative Approach

(1) Humanistic Approach

① Community Language Learning *

a student-centered method that emphasizes the learner's needs and builds a supportive, collaborative environment. It's based on the idea of counseling and learning, where the teacher acts as a "counselor" and the learners are "clients." The method uses the learners' native language as a bridge to the target language, fostering confidence and communication skills.

② Suggestopedia *

a method of teaching a foreign language in which students learn quickly by being made to feel relaxed, interested and positive. The method is developed because of the argument that students naturally face psychological barriers to learning.

③ Silent Way *

a methodology of teaching language based on the idea that teachers should be as silent as possible during a class but learners should be encouraged to speak as much as possible

(2) Comprehension-based Approach

① Total Physical Response **

Instructors give commands to students in the target language with body movements, and students respond with whole-body actions. The method is an example of the comprehension approach to language teaching.

② Audio Motor Unit ***

It includes a particular sequence of commands, all centering on a single topic. The teacher demonstrates the appropriate responses to the commands, using whatever realia are available to make the actions comprehensible. The students are invited to comply with the commands.

③ Natural Approach *

a method of language teaching developed by Stephen Krashen and Tracy Terrell in the late 1970s and early 1980s. It aims to foster naturalistic language acquisition in a classroom setting, and to this end, it emphasizes communication, and places decreased importance on conscious grammar study and explicit correction of student errors.

(3) Lexical Approach

① Lexical Approach **

a language teaching method that emphasized the importance of words/vocabulary in SLA. The lexical approach is a way of analyzing and teaching language based on the idea that a language is made up of lexical units rather than grammatical structures. The units are words, chunks formed by collocations, and fixed phrases.

② Lexicogrammatical Approach ***

A view that lexis and grammar are two inherently connected parts of a single entity and should not be treated separately. Vocabulary and grammatical structures are interdependent; so much so that it is possible to say with some justification that words have their own grammar.

3 Traditional Approach

① Grammar Translation Method *

a language teaching method in which the central focus is on grammatical rules, and vocabulary memorization as the basis for translating from one language to another

② Direct Method *

It emphasizes direct target language use, oral communication skills, and inductive grammar without recourse to translation from the first language.

③ Audio-lingual Method *

a method of foreign language teaching, which emphasizes the teaching of listening and speaking before reading and writing. It is based on behaviorism theory. It uses dialogues as the main form of language presentation and drills as the main training techniques. Mother tongue is discouraged in the classroom.

Apply the Key Terms in Practice

① Teaching Method

Complete the table with the most appropriate terms.

Method	Characteristics	Activities
ⓐ _____ _____	• focus on meaning • focus on functional aspects of language • emphasis on interaction • emphasis on authenticity of input • learner-centered	• collaborative learning through pair and group work; negotiation of meaning • activities focusing on communication • activities focusing on fluency, with a high degree of tolerance for errors • information gap, opinion, and reasoning activities • role play
ⓑ _____ _____	• use of tasks as core units of planning and instruction • use of real-world outcomes	• information gap, jigsaw, problem-solving and other collaborative tasks • communication activities
ⓒ _____ _____	• language learning combined with subject learning • closely tied to learners' needs • importance of comprehension	• performance-oriented activities • discussion activities • collaborative work • meaning-oriented activities
ⓓ _____ _____	• centrality of lexis, particularly multi-word units or chunks • the importance of strategies for learners to deal with chunks	• awareness-raising activities • corpora-based activities • text chunking

ⓔ _____ _____	• focus on the whole person and the affective side of learning • emphasis on providing a safe environment for learning • Learning is a collaborative effort.	• translation (by the teacher, of student messages) • recordings • group work • transcription and analysis • reflection
ⓕ _____ _____	• influence of the unconscious on learning • use of music • teacher-dominant style	• imitation • question and answer • role play • listening practice • music-based activities
ⓖ _____ _____	• focus on giving learners as much opportunities to produce the language in class as possible, in their own • Language learning is seen as problem-solving and discovery learning.	• pronunciation exercises • guided elicitation exercises, followed by practice
ⓗ _____ _____	Learning is supported through body movement.	imperative drills requiring physical responses
ⓘ _____ _____	• strong focus on meaning • lack of explicit instruction on form • emphasis on input over practice • attention to emotional preparedness for learning	• listening activities • acquisition activities focusing on exchange of meaningful information through role play, games, and problem-solving

ⓙ _____ _____	• language taught through speaking • focus on sentence patterns • repetition and drills that lead to habit formation • focus on avoidance of errors and an emphasis on grammatical accuracy	• pronunciation activities • pattern drills • mimicking native-speaking speech • repetition-based tasks
ⓚ _____ _____	focus on oral fluency and conversation ability	• question and answer exercises • conversation practice • reading aloud
ⓛ _____ _____	• focus on vocabulary memorization and grammar rules • translation of passages	• translating reading passages • writing sentences using the new grammar

2 Task-based Instruction

Read the conversation between two teachers and fill in the blanks with the TWO most appropriate words.

Ms. Park : Morning! I've been thinking about our next speaking unit, and I want to end with something authentic for the students.

Mr. Choi : Sounds good. What's your idea?

Ms. Park : For the ⓐ _____, which is a real-world task people actually do outside the classroom, I'm thinking they could fill out an actual online job application for an English-speaking part-time job. They'd need to read the job description, enter their personal details, write a short self-introduction, and upload a résumé.

Mr. Choi : That's definitely something they might do in real life.

Ms. Park : Right. But to prepare them, I'll give them a(n) ⓑ _____, which is a simplified classroom version of that task. They'll practice with a shorter, modified application form–only basic fields like name, contact, work experience, and a two-sentence introduction.

Mr. Choi : That makes sense. It'll help them learn the key language and structure without being overwhelmed.

Ms. Park : Exactly. Once they've done the simplified form, the real online form will feel much easier.

Read the five teachers' perspectives on their lessons. For each one, write the teaching method that best matches the description in the blank.

⬡ **Ms. Park's Perspective – ⓐ** _____

In my beginner English class, I focus on providing lots of **comprehensible input** without forcing students to speak too soon. I create a relaxed environment where they can listen, observe, and understand the meaning before producing language. Grammar instruction is minimal, and accuracy isn't the priority in the early stage. Over time, **as students feel ready, their speech emerges naturally**.

⬡ **Mr. Jung's Perspective – ⓑ** _____

With my young learners, I give clear **commands** like "Stand up," "Open your book," or "Close the window." and they **respond through actions**. Linking language with physical movement keeps the lesson dynamic and memorable. I don't expect verbal responses at first–understanding comes before speaking. Once students feel confident, they start repeating and using the commands themselves.

⬡ **Ms. Yoo's Perspective – ⓒ** _____

In this lesson, I guide students through **a logical sequence of actions while narrating each step in English**. They listen, move, and respond to the cues as part of a structured unit, often set to rhythm or music. This method integrates listening and movement while reinforcing **a specific theme or context**. By repeating the sequence, students internalize both meaning and form without direct grammar drills.

◈ Ms. Lee's Perspective – ⓓ _____

Instead of teaching isolated grammar rules, I focus on exposing students to **high-frequency chunks and collocations**. For example, we learn expressions like "by the way" or "take responsibility for" as whole units. Students notice patterns in authentic texts and practice using these chunks in conversation. Over time, this builds a rich lexical repertoire that supports fluency.

◈ Mr. Choi's Perspective – ⓔ _____

In my lessons, I teach **grammar and vocabulary together as interconnected elements**. For example, when teaching the word "suggest," I also show its common grammatical patterns, like "suggest doing something" or "suggest that + clause." Students practice these in meaningful contexts, so they see how words naturally combine with structures. This helps them **avoid treating vocabulary and grammar as separate subjects**.

Answers

❶ Teaching Method
ⓐ Communicative Language Teaching (CLT)
ⓑ Task-based Language Teaching (TBLT)
ⓒ Content-based Instruction (CBI)
ⓓ Lexical Approach
ⓔ Community Language Learning (CLL)
ⓕ Suggestopedia
ⓖ Silent Way
ⓗ Total Physical Response (TPR)
ⓘ Natural Approach
ⓙ Audiolingual Method (ALM)
ⓚ Direct Method (DM)
ⓛ Grammar Translation Method (GTM)

❷ Task-based Instruction
ⓐ target task
ⓑ pedagogical task

❸ Teacher's Perspectives
ⓐ Natural Approach
ⓑ Total Physical Response
ⓒ Audio-motor Unit
ⓓ Lexical Approach
ⓔ Lexicogrammatical Approach

Learner Variables

Map the Key Terms

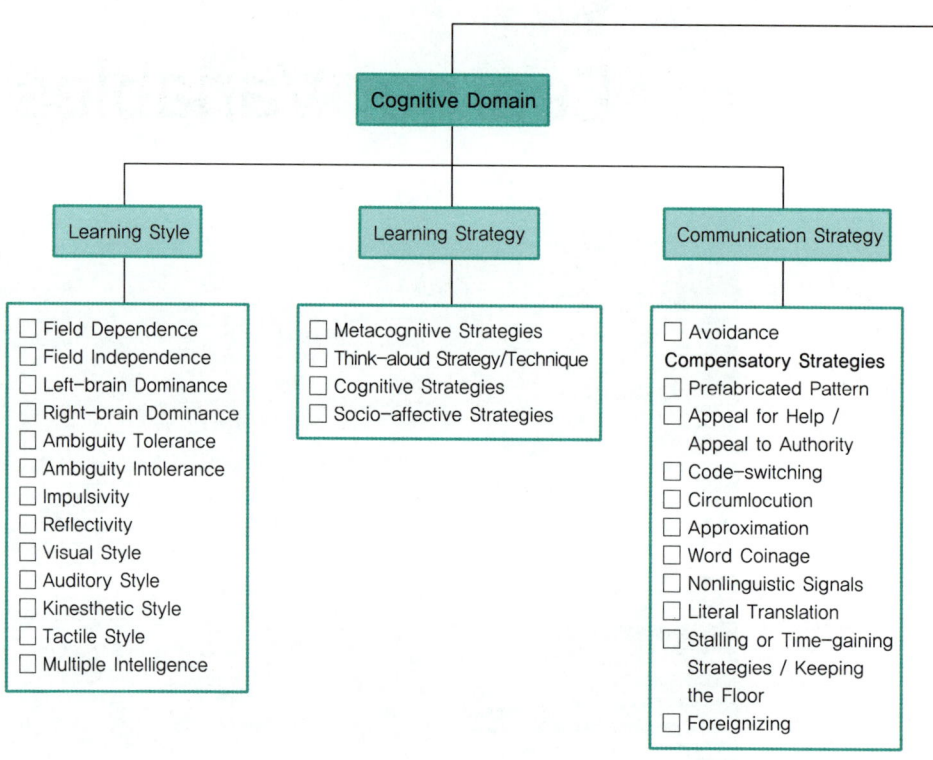

Cognitive Domain

Learning Style

- ☐ Field Dependence
- ☐ Field Independence
- ☐ Left–brain Dominance
- ☐ Right–brain Dominance
- ☐ Ambiguity Tolerance
- ☐ Ambiguity Intolerance
- ☐ Impulsivity
- ☐ Reflectivity
- ☐ Visual Style
- ☐ Auditory Style
- ☐ Kinesthetic Style
- ☐ Tactile Style
- ☐ Multiple Intelligence

Learning Strategy

- ☐ Metacognitive Strategies
- ☐ Think–aloud Strategy/Technique
- ☐ Cognitive Strategies
- ☐ Socio–affective Strategies

Communication Strategy

- ☐ Avoidance
- **Compensatory Strategies**
- ☐ Prefabricated Pattern
- ☐ Appeal for Help / Appeal to Authority
- ☐ Code–switching
- ☐ Circumlocution
- ☐ Approximation
- ☐ Word Coinage
- ☐ Nonlinguistic Signals
- ☐ Literal Translation
- ☐ Stalling or Time–gaining Strategies / Keeping the Floor
- ☐ Foreignizing

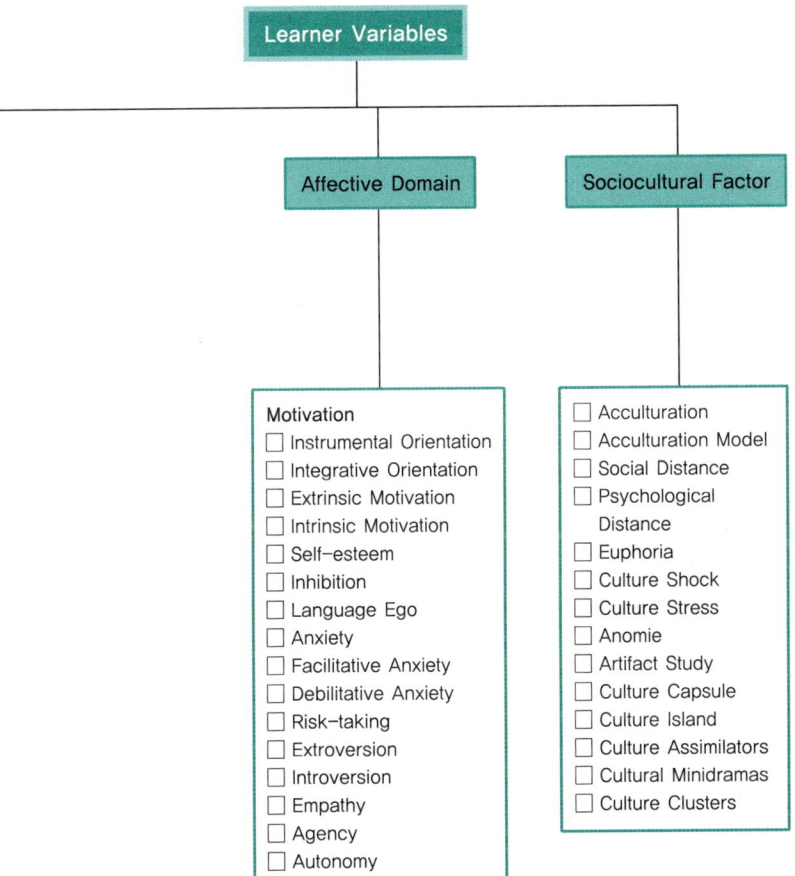

Learner Variables

Affective Domain

Sociocultural Factor

Motivation
- ☐ Instrumental Orientation
- ☐ Integrative Orientation
- ☐ Extrinsic Motivation
- ☐ Intrinsic Motivation
- ☐ Self−esteem
- ☐ Inhibition
- ☐ Language Ego
- ☐ Anxiety
- ☐ Facilitative Anxiety
- ☐ Debilitative Anxiety
- ☐ Risk−taking
- ☐ Extroversion
- ☐ Introversion
- ☐ Empathy
- ☐ Agency
- ☐ Autonomy

- ☐ Acculturation
- ☐ Acculturation Model
- ☐ Social Distance
- ☐ Psychological Distance
- ☐ Euphoria
- ☐ Culture Shock
- ☐ Culture Stress
- ☐ Anomie
- ☐ Artifact Study
- ☐ Culture Capsule
- ☐ Culture Island
- ☐ Culture Assimilators
- ☐ Cultural Minidramas
- ☐ Culture Clusters

1 Cognitive Domain

(1) Learning Style

cognitive, affective, and physiological traits that are relatively stable indicators of how learners perceive, interact with, and respond to the learning environment

① Field Dependence ★★★

the tendency to be "dependent" on the total field so that the parts embedded within the field are not distracting, as you perceive the total field as a unified world

② Field Independence ★★★

ability to perceive a particular, relevant item or factor in a "field" of distracting items

③ Left-brain Dominance ★★

a style that favors logical, analytical thought, with mathematical and linear processing of information

④ Right-brain Dominance ★★

a style in which one favors visual, tactile, and auditory images and is more efficient in processing holistic, integrative, and emotional information

⑤ Ambiguity Tolerance ★★★

a style in which an individual is relatively well suited to withstand or manage a high degree of uncertainty in a linguistic context

⑥ Ambiguity Intolerance ★★★

a style in which an individual is relatively ill-equipped to withstand and manage a high degree of uncertainty in a linguistic context, and as a result may demand more certainty and structure

⑦ Impulsivity ***

an individual's tendency to be comfortable making quick or gambling decisions. Impulsive learners take linguistic risks in the face of possible error and take initiative in conversations.

⑧ Reflectivity ***

an individual's tendency to make slower, more calculated decisions. Reflective learners take time to mentally sort through linguistic complexity and speak only when they are certain about linguistic systems or forms.

⑨ Visual Style ***

the tendency to prefer reading and studying charts, drawings, and other graphic information

⑩ Auditory Style ***

the tendency to prefer listening to lectures and audiotapes

⑪ Kinesthetic Style 기출 ***

the tendency to prefer demonstrations and physical activity involving bodily movement

⑫ Tactile Style ***

a "hands-on" learner who prefers to touch, move, build, or draw what you learn

⑬ Multiple Intelligence ***

the hypothesis that intelligence is not limited to traditional concepts of verbal, logical, and mathematical ability, but has multiple modes including spatial, emotional, musical, contextual, and interpersonal

(2) Learning Strategy

strategic options relating to input, processing, storage, and retrieval, or taking in messages from others

① Metacognitive Strategies ★★★

strategic options that relate to one's "executive" functions; strategies that involve planning for learning, thinking about the learning process as it is taking place, monitoring of one's production or comprehension, and evaluating learning after an activity is completed

② Think-aloud Strategy/Technique 기출 ★★★

Teachers verbalize aloud while reading a selection orally. Their verbalization includes describing things they're doing as they read to monitor their comprehension. The purpose of the think-aloud strategy is to model for students how skilled readers construct meaning from a text.

③ Cognitive Strategies ★★★

strategic options relating to specific learning tasks that involve direct manipulation of the learning material itself: activating knowledge, contextualization, predicting, guessing, inferencing, skimming, scanning

④ Socio-affective Strategies ★★★

strategies that help learners regulate and control emotions, motivations, and attitudes towards learning, as well as help learners learn through contact and interaction with others

(3) Communication Strategy

strategic options relating to output, how one productively expresses meaning, and how one effectively delivers messages to others

① Avoidance 기출 ★★★

avoiding a topic, concept, grammatical construction, or phonological element that poses difficulty

② Compensatory Strategies 기출

- Prefabricated Pattern ★★ : using memorized stock phrases, usually for "survival" purposes
- Appeal for Help / Appeal to Authority ★★★ : asking for aid either directly or indirectly
- Code-switching ★★ : using an L1 word with L1 pronunciation while speaking in L2
- Circumlocution ★★★ : describing an object or idea with a definition
- Approximation ★★★ : using an alternative term which expresses the meaning of the target lexical item as closely as possible
- Word Coinage ★★★ : creating a nonexistent L2 word based on a supposed rule
- Nonlinguistic Signals ★★ : mime, gesture, facial expression, or sound imitation
- Literal Translation ★★ : translating a lexical item, an idiom, or a structure from the learner's L1 to L2
- Stalling or Time-gaining Strategies / Keeping the Floor ★★ : using fillers or hesitation devices to fill pauses and to gain time to think (well, now let's see, uh)
- Foreignizing ★★ : using an L1 word by adjusting it to L2 phonology and/or morphologically

❷ Affective Domain

① Motivation **

- Instrumental Orientation : acquiring a language as a means for attaining instrumental goals, such as acquiring a degree or certificate in an academic institution, furthering a career, reading technical material, translation, etc.
- Integrative Orientation : learning a language in order to integrate oneself into the culture of a second language group and become involved in social interchange in that group
- Extrinsic Motivation : choices made and effort expended on activities in anticipation of a reward from outside and beyond the self
- Intrinsic Motivation : choices made and effort expended on activities for which there is no apparent reward except the activity itself

② Self-esteem **

self-appraisal, self-confidence, knowledge of oneself, usually categorized into "global" (overall), "situational/specific" (in a general context), and "task" (particular activities within a context)

③ Inhibition ***

apprehension over one's self-identity or fear of showing self-doubt, leading to building mechanisms of protective self-defense

④ Language Ego **

the identity a person develops in reference to the language he or she speaks

⑤ Anxiety **

the subjective feeling of tension, apprehension, and nervousness connected to an arousal of the autonomic nervous system, and associated with feelings of uneasiness, frustration, self-doubt, apprehension or worries

⑥ Facilitative Anxiety ***

Facilitative anxiety views stressors as challenges and assists performance. It is the level of anxiety which is perceived as motivating. For instance, perceiving anxiety as facilitative has been found out to be positively associated with academic performance and negatively associated with emotional exhaustion.

⑦ Debilitative Anxiety ***

Debilitative anxiety views stressors as threats and interferes with performance. It is the level of anxiety which is perceived as threatening.

⑧ Risk-taking ***

willingness to gamble, to try out hunches about a language with the possibility of being wrong

⑨ Extroversion **

the extent to which a person has a deep-seated need to receive ego enhancement, self-esteem, and a sense of wholeness from other people as opposed to receiving that affirmation within oneself

⑩ Introversion **

the extent to which a person derives a sense of wholeness and fulfillment within oneself

⑪ Empathy ***

the process of "putting yourself into someone else's shoes" of reaching beyond the self to understand what another person is feeling. Language is one of the primary means of empathizing, but nonverbal communication facilitates the process of empathizing and must not be overlooked. (Note: Empathy and sympathy are not synonymous. Sympathy involves a close affinity with another person while empathy implies more possibility of detachment.)

⑫ Agency **

a person's ability to make choices, take control, self-regulate, and thereby pursue goals as an individual, leading potentially to personal or social transformation

⑬ Autonomy **

individual effort and action through which learners initiate language, problem solving, strategic action, and the generation of linguistic input

❸ Sociocultural Factor

① Acculturation *

a process in which changes in the language, culture, and system of values of a group happen through interaction with another group with a different language, culture, and system of values. For example, in second language learning, acculturation may affect how well one group learns the language of another.

② Acculturation Model *

in second language acquisition, the theory that the rate and level of ultimate success of second language acquisition in naturalistic settings (without instruction) is a function of the degree to which learners acculturate to the target language community. Acculturation may involve a large number of social and psychological variables, but is generally considered to be the process through which an individual takes on the beliefs, values and culture of a new group.

③ Social Distance ***

the perception that learners have of themselves in relation to speakers of the target language

④ Psychological Distance **

It concerns the extent to which individual learners are comfortable with the learning task and constitutes, therefore, a personal rather than a group dimension.

⑤ Euphoria *

the initial stage where individuals feel excitement, enthusiasm, and fascination about the new culture they encounter

⑥ Culture Shock ★★★

in the process of acculturation, phenomena involving mild irritability, depression, anger, or possibly deep psychological crisis due to the foreignness of the new cultural milieu. Culture shock is an experience a person may have when one moves to a cultural environment which is different from one's own; it is also the personal disorientation a person may feel when experiencing an unfamiliar way of life due to immigration or a visit to a new country, a move between social environments, or simply transition to another type of life. One of the most common causes of culture shock involves individuals in a foreign environment. Culture shock can be described as consisting of at least one of four distinct phases: honeymoon, negotiation, adjustment, and adaptation.

⑦ Culture Stress ★★

the ongoing pressure that you live with when you live in another culture or country than the one in which you were raised

⑧ Anomie ★★

feelings of social uncertainty, dissatisfaction, or homelessness as individuals lose some of the bonds of a native culture

⑨ Artifact Study ★★

It is designed to help students discern the cultural significance of certain unfamiliar objects from the target culture. The activity involves students in giving description and forming hypotheses about the function of the unknown object.

⑩ Culture Capsule 기출 ★★★

It is a brief description, usually one or two paragraphs, of some aspect of the target culture, followed by or incorporated with contrasting information about the students' native culture. Culture capsules can be written by teachers or students.

⑪ Culture Island 기출 **

A culture island is an area in the classroom where posters, maps, objects, and pictures of people, lifestyles, or customs of other cultures are displayed to attract learners' attention, evoke comments, and help students develop a mental image.

⑫ Culture Assimilators ***

Students listen to a description or watch an incident of cross-cultural interaction in which miscommunication occurs between a Korean and a member of the target culture. They choose from a list of alternatives an explanation of the episode and finally they read feedback paragraphs that explain whether each alternative is likely and why.

⑬ Cultural Minidramas **

Students listen to, watch, or read a series of episodes in which miscommunication is taking place; each successive episode reveals additional information, with the exact problem in understanding revealed in the last part. Students are led in discussion in order to understand how misunderstandings arise when wrong conclusions are reached about the target culture on the basis of one's own cultural understanding.

⑭ Culture Clusters ***

They consist of illustrated culture capsules, which develop a topic or related topics in a 30-minute classroom simulation, with the information contained in the capsule. The teacher acts as a narrator, guiding the skit through stage directions.

Memo

Apply the Key Terms in Practice

① Individual Learning Style

Read the six students' statements. For each student, write TWO most appropriate learning styles in each blank that best match the description.

⬡ Student 1 – ⓐ _____ Learner

"When the teacher asks a question, I just say the first thing that **pops into my head**, even if I'm not completely sure. If I **don't understand every word** in the reading, I keep going and **try to guess from the context**."

⬡ Student 2 – ⓑ _____ Learner

"I understand better when I **work with classmates to find the main idea** in a reading passage and see how all the details fit together. I **highlight key points** in different colors and use **diagrams** to connect ideas."

⬡ Student 3 – ⓒ _____ Learner

"I remember things best when I can **move around the classroom**–like walking to different stations or acting out a scene. I also like following **a clear, step-by-step process** so I can solve problems **in the right order**."

⬡ Student 4 – ⓓ _____ Learner

"I **study alone** so I can **focus on the details. Writing key words on sticky notes** and moving them around helps me organize ideas and remember them."

⬡ Student 5 – ⓔ _____ Learner

"I learn well when I **hear the teacher tell a story** and *imagine the scenes in my head*. **Hearing** my classmates' ideas during group discussions helps me **connect different ideas into a bigger picture** and **spark my creativity**."

⬡ Student 6 – ⓕ _____ Learner

"If **instructions aren't clear**, I feel **nervous** and **can't start** the task. I usually **plan my answer** in my head **before I speak** in class."

❷ How to Motivate Students

Read the conversation between Ms. Park and Ms. Yoo, and follow the directions.

Ms. Park : Hey, I've been thinking about how to keep our students more motivated in English. Like, Minho keeps saying he wants to do well on the TOEFL Junior test so he can get into a special English program in high school.

Ms. Yoo : Yeah, I've heard him talk about that. We could give him practice tasks similar to the test and some reading passages on topics he's interested in.

Ms. Park : True. And Jiwon–she just gets absorbed in the activities. Last week she stayed after class to finish her own story in English, even though it wasn't homework.

Ms. Yoo : She clearly enjoys the learning process itself. Maybe we could give her more creative projects–like making short comics or skits–so she can explore the language in her own way. What about Sumin?

Ms. Park : Oh, she's really excited about joining the school's sister-school exchange with Australia and making friends there.

Ms. Yoo : Then maybe we can set up pen-pal letters or online meet-ups with the Australian students so she can see a real reason to use English.

Ms. Park : Right. And Hyunsoo–he's been studying a lot harder because his parents promised him a new phone if his grades go up.

Ms. Yoo : For him, short-term goals and quick rewards might be effective. Even giving out "star student" badges in class could help.

Ms. Park : So, I guess figuring out why they're learning makes it so much easier to plan lessons.

Ms. Yoo : Exactly. Match their reason for learning to the right activity, and they're way more likely to stay engaged.

Complete the table by identifying each student's motivation types and briefly stating the reason, based on the conversation above.

Type of Motivation	Student's Name	Evidence from the Conversation
ⓐ _____	Jiwon	ⓔ _____ _____
ⓑ _____	Hyunsoo	ⓕ _____ _____
ⓒ _____	Minho	ⓖ _____ _____
ⓓ _____	Sumin	ⓗ _____ _____

❸ Language Ego and Inhibition

Read the teacher's reflection and fill in each blank with the correct terms.

> 🗁 **Mr. Cho's Reflection**
>
> Today's group discussion on environmental issues really showed how Minji's strong ⓐ _____ influences her learning. She sees herself as a competent English speaker, so her ⓑ _____–the hesitation or fear of making mistakes–is noticeably low. She's quick to volunteer answers without overthinking. This low ⓑ _____ often leads to frequent ⓒ _____. For example, she tried using new vocabulary like *"sustainable"* and *"carbon footprint"*, which we had only introduced this week. Even when she mispronounced *"sustainable"*, she laughed, corrected herself, and kept contributing actively to the discussion. Moments like this remind me how confidence, reduced fear, and willingness to experiment can work together to push a learner's language forward.

4 Acculturation

Read the student's log and fill in each blank with the most appropriate words.

> 📦 Chaewon's Log
>
> When I first arrived in Canada, I think I was in the ⓐ _____ stage. Everything felt new and exciting–the colorful houses, friendly "Hi!" from strangers, and the endless snack choices at the grocery store. Even the school schedule amazed me. I couldn't wait to explore more every day.
>
> After about a month, I started experiencing ⓑ _____. I couldn't understand my classmates' jokes, and group discussions moved so fast that I felt lost. Once, I said, "I will go washroom," and everyone giggled–I didn't even know why until later. I also missed warm rice for lunch instead of cold sandwiches.
>
> Over the next several weeks, I began to feel ⓒ _____. Even after I got used to the school routine, small daily differences kept tiring me out–figuring out unfamiliar slang, remembering to make eye contact with teachers, and trying to laugh at jokes I didn't quite get. These little pressures piled up, and I often felt mentally drained.
>
> By the third month, I realized I was going through ⓓ _____. I didn't fully belong in Canada, but I also didn't feel exactly the same as before. My parents wanted me to speak Korean at home, while my teachers encouraged me to use English at school. I felt caught between two cultures, unsure where I fit.
>
> Now, I think I'm moving toward ⓔ _____. I joined the after-school soccer club and started learning casual English expressions like "no worries" and "my bad." I share Korean snacks with my teammates, and they teach me Canadian slang in return. I've learned that I can still be Korean and feel at home here.

5 Cultural Learning

Read the conversation between two teachers and fill in each blank with the most appropriate teaching technique.

Ms. Kim : You know, I've been thinking–our students are pretty good with grammar and vocab, but they still get stuck when real-life communication involves cultural references.

Mr. Seo : Yeah, I've noticed that too. They can form perfect sentences, but sometimes the meaning gets lost because they don't understand the cultural background.

Ms. Kim : Exactly. That's why I think we need to bring in more cultural learning. If they can recognize the differences between their own culture and the target culture, they'll communicate more naturally.

Mr. Seo : True. How about starting with something like a(n) ⓐ _____?

Ms. Kim : That could work. Remind me–how would you set that up in class?

Mr. Seo : I'd present **a short description or visuals about a specific aspect of the target culture**–say, how birthdays are celebrated in Canada. Then, students would **compare it** to how birthdays are celebrated in Korea. They could write a short paragraph or do a quick discussion on **similarities and differences**.

Ms. Kim : I like that–it's clear and focused. But what about situations where cultural misunderstanding might happen?

Mr. Seo : That's where a(n) ⓑ _____ comes in. I'd give them a short scenario **where a misunderstanding occurs**–for example, a Korean student in the U.S. thinks their host is being rude because they didn't offer food multiple times. Students read the scenario, then **choose the most likely explanation from several options**. After that, we'd discuss why that's the correct one.

Ms. Kim : Nice. That way, they're not just learning facts but actually practicing interpreting cultural behavior.

Answers

1 Individual Learning Style

ⓐ Impulsive & Ambiguity Tolerant
ⓑ Field Dependent & Visual
ⓒ Kinesthetic & Left-brain Dominant
ⓓ Field Independent & Tactile
ⓔ Right-brain Dominant & Auditory
ⓕ Ambiguity Intolerant & Reflective

2 How to Motivate Students

ⓐ Intrinsic motivation
ⓑ Extrinsic motivation
ⓒ Instrumental motivation
ⓓ Integrative motivation
ⓔ stayed after class to finish her own story in English, even though it's not homework.
ⓕ studying a lot harder because his parents promised him a new phone if his grades go up.
ⓖ wants to do well on the TOEFL Junior test to get into a special English program in high school.
ⓗ excited about joining the school's sister-school exchange with Australia and making friends there.

3 Language Ego and Inhibition

ⓐ language ego
ⓑ inhibition
ⓒ risk taking

4 Acculturation

ⓐ euphoria
ⓑ culture shock
ⓒ culture stress
ⓓ anomie
ⓔ acculturation

5 Cultural Learning

ⓐ culture capsule
ⓑ culture assimilator

Coursework Design

Map the Key Terms

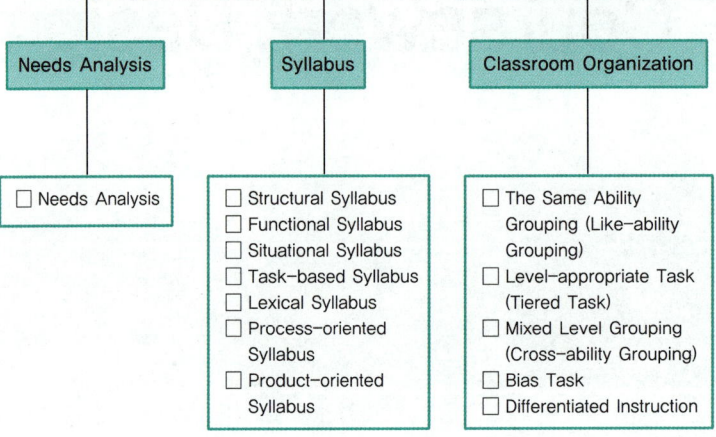

Needs Analysis	Syllabus	Classroom Organization
☐ Needs Analysis	☐ Structural Syllabus ☐ Functional Syllabus ☐ Situational Syllabus ☐ Task-based Syllabus ☐ Lexical Syllabus ☐ Process-oriented Syllabus ☐ Product-oriented Syllabus	☐ The Same Ability Grouping (Like-ability Grouping) ☐ Level-appropriate Task (Tiered Task) ☐ Mixed Level Grouping (Cross-ability Grouping) ☐ Bias Task ☐ Differentiated Instruction

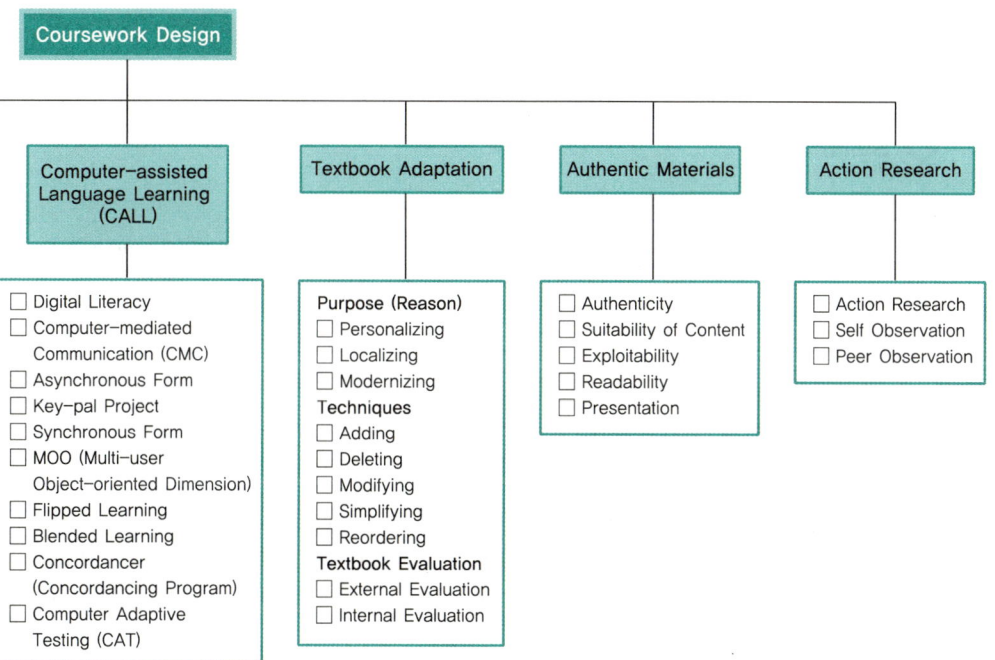

Coursework Design

Computer-assisted Language Learning (CALL)

☐ Digital Literacy
☐ Computer-mediated Communication (CMC)
☐ Asynchronous Form
☐ Key-pal Project
☐ Synchronous Form
☐ MOO (Multi-user Object-oriented Dimension)
☐ Flipped Learning
☐ Blended Learning
☐ Concordancer (Concordancing Program)
☐ Computer Adaptive Testing (CAT)

Textbook Adaptation

Purpose (Reason)
☐ Personalizing
☐ Localizing
☐ Modernizing
Techniques
☐ Adding
☐ Deleting
☐ Modifying
☐ Simplifying
☐ Reordering
Textbook Evaluation
☐ External Evaluation
☐ Internal Evaluation

Authentic Materials

☐ Authenticity
☐ Suitability of Content
☐ Exploitability
☐ Readability
☐ Presentation

Action Research

☐ Action Research
☐ Self Observation
☐ Peer Observation

Master the Key Terms

❶ Needs Analysis

① Needs Analysis 기출 ★★★

Needs analysis is the process of specifying the learners' language needs in advance of designing a course of them. The analysis can then be used to materials, and also the methodology. Finally, the needs analysis can be used in the design of assessment and evaluation procedures.

❷ Syllabus

① Structural Syllabus ★★★

a language course that attends primarily to forms (grammar, phonology, lexicon) as organizing elements of a foreign language curriculum

② Functional Syllabus ★★★

a language course that attends primarily to functions as organizing elements of a foreign language curriculum

③ Situational Syllabus ★★★

This contains a collection of real or imaginary situations in which language occurs or is used. It usually involves several participants who are engaged in some activities in a specific setting. The primary purpose is to teach the language that occurs in the situations.

④ Task-based Syllabus 기출 ★★★

This does not organize the teaching with the linguistics features of the language being learned. It contains a series of complex and purposeful tasks that the students want or need to perform with the language they are learning.

⑤ Lexical Syllabus ★★

a type of language course design that organizes learning content around high-frequency words, lexical chunks, and collocations

⑥ Process-oriented Syllabus ★★★

the syllabus focusing on the skills and processes involved in learning language

⑦ Product-oriented Syllabus **

the syllabus focusing on things learned at the end of the learning process/outcomes

❸ Classroom Organization

① The Same Ability Grouping (Like-ability Grouping) ***

The same ability grouping involves placing students with similar levels together. This allows teachers to tailor instruction and activities to the group's shared proficiency, providing appropriate pacing and targeted support.

② Level-appropriate Task (Tiered Task) **

designing tasks at different levels of difficulty to match students' varying ability. All students work toward the same learning goal but complete tasks suited to their readiness levels.

③ Mixed Level Grouping (Cross-ability Grouping) ***

This means forming groups with students of different ability levels. This encourages peer support and collaboration, allowing higher-level students to help lower-level peers, and promoting mutual learning.

④ Bias Task **

This involves intentionally designing activities with varying levels of complexity or open-endedness within the same task, so that all students can participate and achieve success regardless of their individual ability level.

cf Differentiated Instruction ***

This is about taking account of significant differences among students in terms of their ability, rate of learning, language proficiency, literacy and numeracy skills— and then using this knowledge to adapt the way the curriculum and learning activities are presented.

4 Computer-Assisted Language Learning (CALL)

① Digital Literacy ★★★

It is the ability to understand and use information in multiple formats from a wide variety of sources when it is presented via computers.

② Computer-mediated Communication (CMC) ★★

communication through the use of two or more electronic devices such as computers, tablet PCs, and smart phones. Commonly used formats are e-mail, video, audio, or text chatting supported by social software.

③ Asynchronous Form ★★

This involves communication where participants do not need to be online at the same time. It allows more time for reflection and composing responses.

④ Key-pal Project ★★

Keypals are the term for pen pals who use email to communicate and provide a simple and effective way of putting learners in touch with other learners in other parts of the world. Learners can talk about their experiences of learning English, and email is the perfect medium for cross-cultural communication.

⑤ Synchronous Form ★★

This refers to real-time communication where participants interact at the same time. It allows immediate feedback and a more spontaneous, conversational flow.

⑥ MOO (Multi-user Object-oriented Dimension) ★

It is a permanent space on the Internet set aside for a specific group, a virtual environment. You could call it an online community.

⑦ Flipped Learning 기출 ★★★

This is a pedagogical model in which the typical lecture and homework elements of a course are reversed. There is a divide between the technology and face-to-face elements of the learning experience. A learner is asked to watch an e-Learning video or participate in another online learning exercise before coming to class. In the classroom the new materials are explored at-length. In most cases, the knowledge that is learned online is applied in the classroom.

⑧ Blended Learning **

This involves online and face-to-face instruction. Both are used alongside each other in order to provide a comprehensive learning experience. For example, a trainer might give learners a list of online resources they can use to broaden their understanding of the topic, or ask them to complete an online group project that centers on a subject they are currently discussing. In the case of blended learning, online materials do not take the place of face-to-face instruction; instead, the two modalities complement one another. They truly "blend" in order to create an enriched online training environment for the learner.

⑨ Concordancer (Concordancing Program) ***

It is a software tool used to search large collections of texts and generate a list of all occurrences of a particular word or phrase along with its immediate context. It helps researchers and language learners analyze word usage patterns, collocations, and grammatical structure.

⑩ Computer Adaptive Testing (CAT) 기출 ***

a test administered by computer in which the difficulty level of the next item to be presented to test takers is estimated on the basis of their responses to previous items and adapted to match their abilities

Chapter 04

⑤ Textbook Adaptation

① Purpose (Reason) 기출 ★★

- Personalizing: adapting textbook content to match students' individual interests, experiences, or needs
- Localizing: modifying textbook content to reflect the local context of the learners
- Modernizing: updating textbook content to include current topics, contemporary language use, or up-to-date cultural references

② Techniques 기출 ★★★

- Adding: to add necessary materials by expanding or extending
- Deleting: omission of some exercises or materials by subtracting or abridging
- Modifying: rewriting to change the content, or restructuring to change the way the task is carried out in class
- Simplifying: rewording or paraphrasing the text without damaging its authenticity
- Reordering: the possibility of putting the parts of a course book in a different order. This may mean adjusting the sequence of presentation within a unit, or taking units in a different sequence from that originally intended.

③ Textbook Evaluation ★

- External Evaluation: External evaluation is concerned to obtain a general impression of the material; wide-ranging but relatively superficial.
- Internal Evaluation: In-depth techniques go beneath the publisher's and author's claims to look at.

6 Authentic Materials

① Authenticity 기출 ★★★

how closely a text or material resembles real-life language use as it naturally occurs outside the classroom

② Suitability of Content ★★★

The reading material should interest the students as well as be relevant to their needs. The texts should be motivating.

③ Exploitability ★★★

It refers to how the text can be used to develop the students' competence as readers.

④ Readability ★★★

It is used to describe the combination of the structural and lexical difficulty of a text, as well as referring to the amount of new vocabulary and any new grammatical forms.

⑤ Presentation ★★

The physical or visual presentation of the material should be clear and attractive.

7 Action Research

① Action Research 기출 ★★★

the systematic investigation of an issue, problem, or pedagogical question in a 'live' classroom setting with students, and reporting on the findings of the investigation. It is conducted by L2 teachers in their own classrooms in order to address questions that are particularly relevant to their own teaching contexts. It is often viewed as an iterative process in which teachers identify a topic of investigation related to their teaching, evaluate this topic, and then modify their teaching in light of their findings. (Four steps: planning, acting, observing, and reflecting)

② Self Observation ★★

the process in which teachers systematically reflect on and analyze their own teaching practices by recording, taking notes, or using checklists

③ Peer Observation ★★

Teachers observe each other's classes to provide constructive feedback and share effective teaching strategies.

Memo

Apply the Key Terms in Practice

① Needs Analysis

Read the conversation between two middle school English teachers, and fill in the blanks with the most appropriate terms in common.

Ms. Kim : Before we start planning the coursework for next semester, I think we should first conduct a(n) _____.

Mr. Lee : I agree. Without understanding what our students **need, want, and lack**, we might end up designing a course that doesn't really fit their goals.

Ms. Kim : Exactly. _____ helps us figure out not only their **target needs**–what they need to do with English–but also their **learning needs**–how they prefer to learn.

Mr. Lee : Right. For example, some students may want to improve their speaking fluency, while others may need to develop reading comprehension for exams. If we don't analyze these needs, we could end up providing the wrong focus.

Ms. Kim : And we also have to consider students' **present situation**. Their proficiency levels, learning backgrounds, and even their motivation can really influence how effective our coursework will be.

Mr. Lee : True. Gathering data from **surveys, interviews, and diagnostic tests** will give us a clearer picture. Once we have that, we can prioritize learning objectives and choose materials that actually meet students' goals.

Ms. Kim : Exactly my point. _____ isn't just a formality–it's the foundation for creating a meaningful and **learner-centered** course design.

Mr. Lee : Then let's plan our first step as designing a simple questionnaire for students. That'll give us useful insights before we dive into the syllabus design.

2 Syllabus (1)

Read the five teachers' comments and fill in each blank with the most appropriate syllabus type.

> 🔹 **Ms. Kim** – ⓐ _____
>
> I plan my lessons in **a very clear sequence of grammar points**. For example, we start with *simple present, then move to past tense, then present perfect*, and so on. Each unit focuses on **one structure at a time**, and students practice it until they can use it accurately. I believe mastering the form step-by-step makes everything else easier.
>
> 🔹 **Mr. Kang** – ⓑ _____
>
> I choose situations students are likely to face–like *visiting a doctor, ordering at a café, or checking in at an airport*. Each lesson gives them the **vocabulary and phrases for that situation** and we practice them through dialogues and role plays. The content makes the language easier to remember and more relevant to their lives.
>
> 🔹 **Ms. Yoo** – ⓒ _____
>
> I don't organize lessons by grammar rules–I organize them by **what students need to do in real life**. One week, the goal might be *making polite requests*; another week, it's *giving directions or apologizing*. I teach the expressions and patterns that fit each function, and we role-play so students can use them right away in authentic situations.

Chapter **04**

⬡ Mr. Park – ⓓ _____

In my class, the main goal isn't to 'study' the language–it's to **complete tasks** that require English. For example, students might work together *to plan a holiday, solve a problem in a community, or create a class magazine*. They naturally use the vocabulary and grammar they need while focusing on getting the task done successfully.

⬡ Ms. Jung – ⓔ _____

In today's lesson I focused on **high-frequency vocabulary** related to *shopping and money (price, cheap, expensive, try on, cashier, discount)*. We began with a short dialogue from the textbook, highlighting target words in context. Students worked in pairs to match vocabulary items with pictures and definitions.

3 Syllabus (2)

Below is a comparative syllabus table for middle school English teachers and the short summary. Fill in the blanks with the most appropriate syllabus types.

Syllabus Type	Main Focus	Organizing Principle	Typical Lesson Goal	Example Activity (Middle School)
ⓐ _____ _____	Grammar structures and sentence patterns	Sequence of grammatical items (simple → complex)	Mastery of a specific grammatical form	Present perfect through explanation, drills, and sentence-making
ⓑ _____ _____	Language functions (what people do with language)	Functions like requesting, apologizing, giving opinions	Use language appropriately in common situations	Role-play: Students practice asking for and giving directions.
ⓒ _____ _____	Real-life situations	Topics/settings such as "at the restaurant," "at the doctor's"	Use relevant language in a specific context	Dialogue practice: Ordering food at a café
ⓓ _____ _____	Completing meaningful tasks	Tasks that require communication to achieve an outcome	Communicate effectively to accomplish the task	Group task(project): Plan a weekend trip and present itinerary.

Chapter 04

	Vocabulary and common collocations	High-frequency words, chunks, and phrases	Build vocabulary for fluent and natural communication	Matching game: Pair words and collocations like make a decision, take a break
ⓔ _____ _____				

⬡ Key Distinctions at a Glance

Structural = ⓕ _____-**first** (focus on grammar rules)

Functional = ⓖ _____-**first** (what you want to achieve with language)

Situational = ⓗ _____-**first** (where/when you use it)

Task-Based = ⓘ _____-**first** (complete a communicative goal)

Lexical = ⓙ _____-**first** (what vocabulary and chunks you need)

4 Grouping

Read the conversation between two teachers and fill in the blanks with the most appropriate terms.

Ms. Kim : I'm planning a speaking lesson for my second-year students next week.

Mr. Lee : How will you group them?

Ms. Kim : I'm thinking of ⓐ _____ grouping.

Mr. Lee : Why that approach?

Ms. Kim : It lets me use ⓑ _____ tasks so each group gets materials at the right difficulty level.

Mr. Lee : So you can give beginners more structured prompts and advanced groups open-ended ones?

Ms. Kim : Exactly. It also makes students feel more comfortable–no one feels intimidated by much stronger classmates.

Mr. Lee : That sounds well-structured. I usually go for ⓒ _____ grouping instead.

Ms. Kim : What's the benefit there?

Mr. Lee : Lower-level students get exposure to richer language, and higher-level ones deepen their understanding by explaining ideas. It promotes peer scaffolding.

Ms. Kim : I see.

Mr. Lee : I'm using a jigsaw as a(n) ⓓ _____ task. In each ⓒ _____ group, students will get different amounts of information based on their proficiency level, so that everyone can contribute at their own level but still depend on each other to complete the task.

Ms. Kim : Good point. ⓐ _____ grouping supports differentiated instruction, while ⓒ _____ grouping promotes peer learning across proficiency levels.

Mr. Lee : Exactly. It really depends on the learning goal.

5 Technology-Based Learning

Read each student's reflection about their English class experience and follow the directions.

⬡ Suji

Our class meets twice a week in person, and between lessons we complete online grammar and vocabulary work. Last week I studied conditionals at home through an interactive lecture and quiz, then used them in pair dialogues in class. It's flexible, but I sometimes miss deadlines for the online part.

⬡ Sungjin

We study new topics before class by watching short videos and reading slides. Before our persuasive essay lesson, I watched a video on thesis statements, then in class we moved straight to peer editing. Preparing in advance makes the activities easier, but skipping it leaves me lost.

⬡ Jinyoung

Last week, we took an online reading test that adjusted the questions depending on my answers. When I got a question about a short news article correctly, the next question was a more complex academic text. When I struggled with that one, the following question was slightly easier. It was strange not knowing how difficult the next item would be, but I liked how the test seemed to match my level. It felt more precise than a paper test where everyone gets the same set of questions.

⬡ Soyoung

For our vocabulary project, we used an online tool that searches real-life examples of how a word is used. I typed in 'take responsibility' and saw dozens of sentences from newspapers, novels, and blogs. I noticed it was often followed by 'for' plus a noun, like 'take responsibility for the mistake.' At first, all the sentences felt overwhelming to read, but the patterns became clearer, and I started using the phrase more naturally in my writing.

Based on the four students' reflections, complete the table by identifying appropriate technology-based learning approach or tool for each student and write the supporting phrases from the reflection.

Student	Technology-based Learning	Supporting Phrases from the Reflection
Suji	ⓐ _____	ⓔ _____ _____
Sungjin	ⓑ _____	ⓕ _____ _____
Jinyoung	ⓒ _____	ⓖ _____ _____
Soyoung	ⓓ _____	ⓗ _____ _____

6 Criteria for Choosing Text

Read the conversation between two teachers and fill in the blanks with the most appropriate terms.

Two English teachers are selecting a reading text for their second-grade class.

Ms. Kim : We need to pick a text for next week's second-grade reading lesson. Between Text A, the *National Geographic* article, and Text B, the travel blog, which one seems better?

Mr. Park : In terms of ⓐ _____, I like that both texts are from real-world sources. It's good for students to experience natural English rather than simplified textbook passages.

Ms. Kim : I agree. But I'm a bit concerned about ⓑ _____. Text A has longer sentences and several technical terms about environmental science. That might be too challenging for some of our students.

Mr. Park : True, Text B is written in a more conversational tone. The sentences are shorter, and the vocabulary is easier, which could make it less intimidating for lower-level learners.

Ms. Kim : That's right. But we also need to think about ⓒ _____. Text A connects directly to the students' science unit on environmental issues, so it could feel more meaningful. Text B is fun, but I'm not sure all students would relate to a hiking story.

Mr. Park : Good point. If we choose Text A, we'll need to support students who might struggle with its complexity. We could pre-teach key vocabulary, provide a short glossary, or highlight important sentences to make it more accessible.

Ms. Kim : I like that idea. We could also chunk the text into smaller sections and give students guiding questions for each part. That should make the passage less overwhelming while keeping the original content.

Mr. Park : Exactly. And when it comes to ⓓ _____, Text A gives us far more options. We can design vocabulary tasks, comprehension exercises, critical thinking questions, and even a short debate about environmental solutions. With Text B, there aren't as many details to build activities around.

Ms. Kim : Agreed. As long as we prepare some scaffolding to handle the readability issue, Text A seems like the better fit overall.

Mr. Park : Perfect. Let's go with Text A and plan some pre-reading activities to support the students.

7 Textbook Adaptation

Read each student's review about a specific chapter from their textbook and follow the directions.

⬡ Students' Reviews on the Textbook

Chapter 2

By Jiwon   : The role-play came at the start of the chapter, before I learned the key vocabulary. I didn't know what to say, so I had to keep looking at the glossary. It would make more sense to do the activity after learning the vocabulary and reading the text.

Chapter 3

By Sujin   : The listening activity was done as a whole-class exercise, and there was no chance to discuss answers in pairs or small groups. I found it hard to stay focused because I wasn't actively involved. If the activity were adjusted to include more interaction, like pair or group work, I think I could participate more and understand the content better.

Chapter 4

By Junhyung : The reading passage was quite short and had only a few examples. When I moved on to the speaking task, I didn't have enough ideas to share. If the book had more examples or extra activities, I think I could have joined the discussion with more confidence.

Chapter 5

By Kyungmin : The idiom section had a long list of idioms, but many of them were too difficult and not very useful for everyday conversation. I spent so much time trying to learn them that I couldn't finish the other activities I wish the chapter focused more on words I can use right away.

Chapter 6

By Hana   : The reading passage used long sentences and difficult expressions, and the examples were hard to relate to. Even though the ideas were correct, the way they were expressed made it hard for me to understand. If the same content were reworded with simpler language and replaced with examples from everyday situations, I think I could understand it more clearly while keeping the main message of the text.

Based on the problem described, write the most appropriate textbook adaptation technique in the blank provided in the table.

Chapter Number	Adaptation Technique
Chapter 2	ⓐ _____
Chapter 3	ⓑ _____
Chapter 4	ⓒ _____
Chapter 5	ⓓ _____
Chapter 6	ⓔ _____

8 Action Research

Read the Ms. Yoo's reflection and fill in the blanks with the most appropriate terms.

🔲 Ms. Yoo's Reflection

   Last semester, I decided to carry out ⓐ _____ to address a recurring problem in my English class. During group work, I noticed that some students dominated the discussion while others stayed silent. My goal was to create more balanced participation and clearer role distribution.

   As part of the data collection, I began with ⓑ _____. I recorded three of my lessons and analyzed how I gave instructions, assigned roles, and monitored groups. I realized that my instructions were sometimes too general, and I rarely checked if every student had a role.

   I also asked a colleague to conduct ⓒ _____ during one lesson. She pointed out that I tended to focus on the more active groups and unintentionally overlooked quieter students. This feedback helped me see patterns I had missed in my own recordings.

   Based on these findings, I made specific changes: I assigned roles before each task, provided clear role cards, and monitored each group more evenly. In the following weeks, I noticed more students contributing to discussions, and the overall quality of group work improved. Through this process, I learned that ⓐ _____ is not just about identifying problems but also about making small, targeted changes and observing their effects over time.

Answers

1 Needs Analysis

needs analysis / Needs analysis

2 Syllabus (1)

ⓐ Structural Syllabus
ⓑ Situational Syllabus
ⓒ Functional Syllabus
ⓓ Task-based Syllabus
ⓔ Lexical Syllabus

3 Syllabus (2)

ⓐ Structural Syllabus
ⓑ Functional Syllabus
ⓒ Situational Syllabus
ⓓ Task-based Syllabus
ⓔ Lexical Syllabus
ⓕ form
ⓖ purpose
ⓗ context
ⓘ goal
ⓙ word

4 Grouping

ⓐ same-ability / Same-ability
ⓑ tiered
ⓒ mixed-level
ⓓ bias

5 Technology-Based Learning

ⓐ Blended Learning
ⓑ Flipped Learning
ⓒ Computerized-adaptive Testing
ⓓ Concordancer
ⓔ in person, online grammar and vocabulary work
ⓕ before class by watching short videos and reading slides, in class we moved straight to peer editing, Preparing in advance
ⓖ adjusted the questions depending on my answers, match my level
ⓗ searches real-life examples of how a word is used, saw dozens of sentences

6 Criteria for Choosing Text

ⓐ authenticity
ⓑ readability
ⓒ suitability of content
ⓓ exploitability

7 Textbook Adaptation

ⓐ Reordering
ⓑ Modifying
ⓒ Adding
ⓓ Deleting
ⓔ Simplifying

8 Action Research

ⓐ action research
ⓑ self observation
ⓒ peer observation

Chapter 04

Receptive Skills

Map the Key Terms

Receptive Skills → Common Characteristics

- [ ] Schema
- [ ] Low-level Schemata
- [ ] High-level Schemata
- [ ] Content Schemata
- [ ] Formal Schemata
- [ ] Linguistic Schemata
- [ ] Contextual Knowledge
- [ ] Extralinguistic Knowledge
- [ ] Microskills
- [ ] Macroskills

Comprehension Level

- [ ] Literal Comprehension
- [ ] Inferential Comprehension
- [ ] Critical Comprehension
- [ ] Appreciative Comprehension
- [ ] Applied Comprehension

Comprehension Process

- [ ] Bottom-up Processing
- [ ] Top-down Processing

Comprehension Process

- [ ] Bottom-up Processing
- [ ] Top-down Processing
- [ ] Interactive Processing

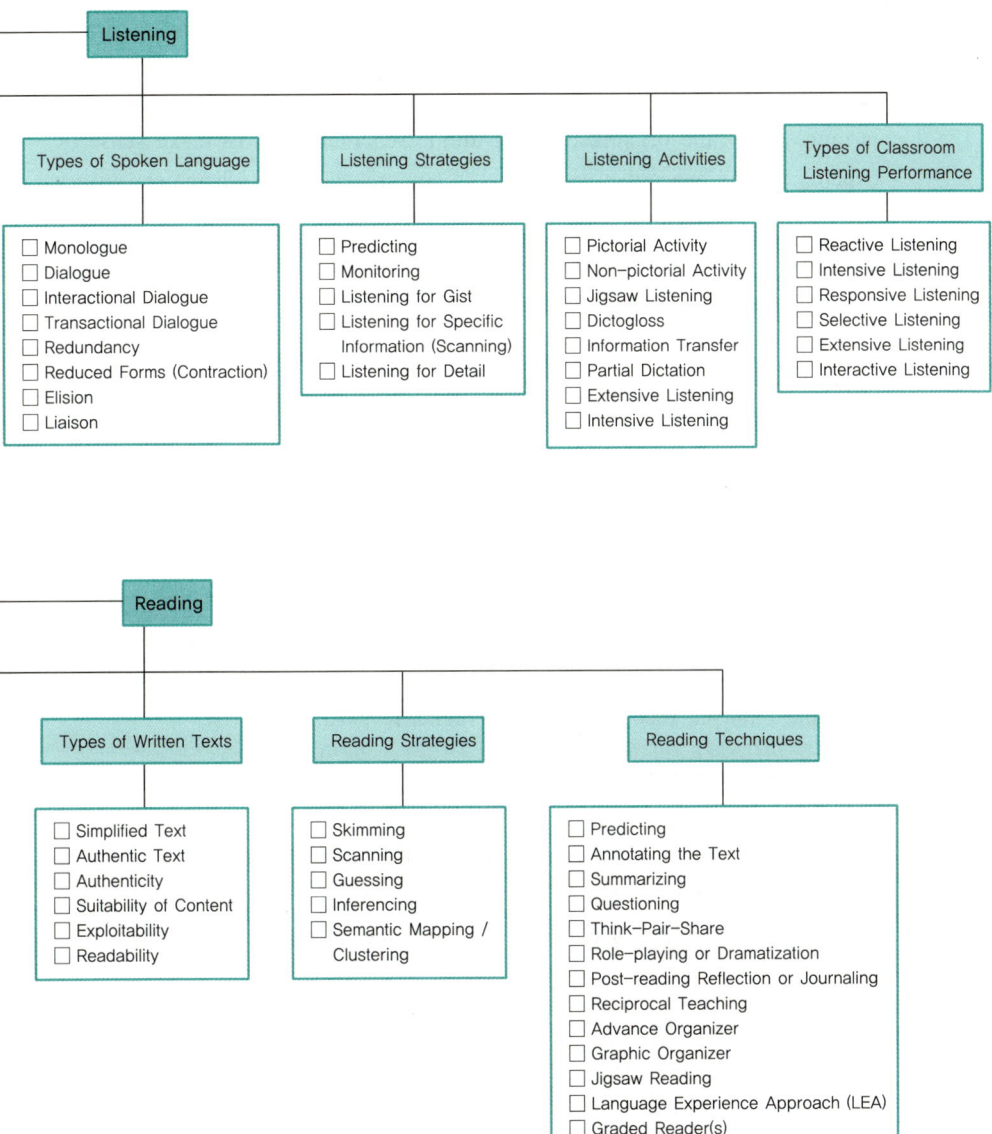

Listening

Types of Spoken Language
- ☐ Monologue
- ☐ Dialogue
- ☐ Interactional Dialogue
- ☐ Transactional Dialogue
- ☐ Redundancy
- ☐ Reduced Forms (Contraction)
- ☐ Elision
- ☐ Liaison

Listening Strategies
- ☐ Predicting
- ☐ Monitoring
- ☐ Listening for Gist
- ☐ Listening for Specific Information (Scanning)
- ☐ Listening for Detail

Listening Activities
- ☐ Pictorial Activity
- ☐ Non-pictorial Activity
- ☐ Jigsaw Listening
- ☐ Dictogloss
- ☐ Information Transfer
- ☐ Partial Dictation
- ☐ Extensive Listening
- ☐ Intensive Listening

Types of Classroom Listening Performance
- ☐ Reactive Listening
- ☐ Intensive Listening
- ☐ Responsive Listening
- ☐ Selective Listening
- ☐ Extensive Listening
- ☐ Interactive Listening

Reading

Types of Written Texts
- ☐ Simplified Text
- ☐ Authentic Text
- ☐ Authenticity
- ☐ Suitability of Content
- ☐ Exploitability
- ☐ Readability

Reading Strategies
- ☐ Skimming
- ☐ Scanning
- ☐ Guessing
- ☐ Inferencing
- ☐ Semantic Mapping / Clustering

Reading Techniques
- ☐ Predicting
- ☐ Annotating the Text
- ☐ Summarizing
- ☐ Questioning
- ☐ Think-Pair-Share
- ☐ Role-playing or Dramatization
- ☐ Post-reading Reflection or Journaling
- ☐ Reciprocal Teaching
- ☐ Advance Organizer
- ☐ Graphic Organizer
- ☐ Jigsaw Reading
- ☐ Language Experience Approach (LEA)
- ☐ Graded Reader(s)
- ☐ Basal Readers
- ☐ Extensive Reading
- ☐ Sustained Silent Reading
- ☐ Intensive Reading

Master the Key Terms

❶ Common Characteristics

① Schema 기출 ★★★

A schema (plural *schemata*) is the way that knowledge about a topic or a concept is represented and organized in the mind. Schemata help us make sense of experience, and hence they are crucial in comprehension. A schema constitutes part of what is called the top-down knowledge of a text. If students do not have the schema, or if the schema is represented differently in their own culture, or if they simply fail to access it, they will have to rely on bottom-up processing alone. Thus, the teachers can help learners understand a text by priming them to activate the appropriate schema. One way of doing this is to use contextual information, such as titles, headlines, pictures, as clues as to what the text is about. Another is to ask them to brainstorm what they already know about a topic.

② Low-level Schemata ★

A low-level schema refers to schemata that are automatically activated at the sensory or surface level. These schemata help process specific, detailed language information, such as word forms, sounds, or grammatical structures. They are closely related to bottom-up (data-driven) processing, in which smaller units are recognized first and then integrated into higher-level structures.

③ High-level Schemata ★

A high-level schema refers to schemata that involve more abstract, global knowledge structures, such as discourse patterns, genre conventions, and cultural context. They are associated with top-down (conceptually driven) processing, where overall meaning or expectations guide the interpretation of lower-level details.

④ Content Schemata ★★★

A content schema refers to background knowledge of the content area of the text. It contains conceptual knowledge or information about what usually happens within a certain topic, and how these happenings relate to each other to form a coherent whole. It is an open-ended set of typical events and entities for a specific occasion.

⑤ Formal Schemata ***

A formal schema refers to background knowledge of the formal, rhetorical organizational structures of different types of texts. In other words, it refers to the knowledge of the ways in which different genres are presented.

⑥ Linguistic Schemata **

A linguistic schema refers to the knowledge about vocabulary and grammar. It plays a basic role in a comprehensive understanding of the text.

⑦ Contextual Knowledge **

For receptive skills, prior and shared knowledge involve both schematic and contextual knowledge. Schematic knowledge consists of both content schemata and formal schemata.

- (Related to listening) listener's overall sense of the situation regarding the participants, the setting, the topic, and the purpose
- (Related to reading) Readers should consider the title and subtitles of the text, the author's background, and the larger context in which the text appeared.

Chapter 05

⑧ Extralinguistic Knowledge *

This refers to background knowledge beyond the language itself, including cultural, social, and situational context. It helps listeners or readers interpret meaning more fully by considering factors like the speaker's intention, cultural norms, or real-world references.

⑨ Microskills *

skills that are at the sentence level

⑩ Macroskills *

skills that are technically at the discourse level

⑪ Comprehension Level

- Literal Comprehension *******: Literal comprehension involves understanding the explicit meaning of the text—what is directly stated. At this level, students focus on factual information and details without interpreting or inferring beyond what is clearly mentioned.

- Inferential Comprehension *******: Inferential comprehension goes beyond the literal meaning and requires students to "read between the lines" by making inferences based on context, clues, and background knowledge. Students must derive meaning that is not explicitly stated in the text.

- Critical Comprehension *******: Critical comprehension requires students to evaluate and analyze the text, assess the credibility of information, detect bias, and form their own judgments or opinions about the material. This level engages students' higher-order thinking skills.

- Appreciative Comprehension ******: Appreciative comprehension involves an emotional or aesthetic response to a text. At this level, students interpret and value the language, style, tone, and the author's creative use of language. This often occurs when engaging with literature, poetry, or narratives.

- Applied Comprehension ******: Applied comprehension requires students to take what they have learned from a text and apply it to real-world situations or new contexts. This level of comprehension connects the text with practical experiences, encouraging students to synthesize information and use it in different scenarios.

❷ Listening

(1) Comprehension Process

① Bottom-up Processing 기출 ★★

This proceeds from sounds to words to grammatical relationships to lexical meanings, and so on, to a final "message." Bottom-up techniques typically focus on the "bits and pieces" of language, breaking language into component parts and giving them central focus.

② Top-down Processing 기출 ★★

This is evoked from "a bank of prior knowledge and global expectations" and other background information (schemata) that the listener brings to the text. Top-down techniques are more concerned with the activation of schemata, with deriving meaning, with global understanding, and with the interpretation of a text.

(2) Types of Spoken Language

① Monologue ★

When one speaker uses spoken language for any length of time, as in speeches, lectures, readings, news broadcasts, and the like, the hearer must process long stretches of speech without interruption—the stream of speech will go on whether or not the hearer comprehends.

② Dialogue ★

It involves two or more speakers and can be subdivided into those exchanges that promote social relationships (interpersonal) and those for which the purpose is to convey propositional or factual information (transactional). In each case, participants may have a good deal of shared knowledge (background knowledge, schemata); therefore, the familiarity of the interlocutors will produce conversations with more assumptions, implications, and other meanings hidden between the lines.

③ Interactional Dialogue 기출 ★★★

The primary focus is on social interaction between the speaker and the need to communicate such things as rapport, empathy, interest and social harmony. Interactional communication is primarily person-orientated.

④ Transactional Dialogue 기출 ★★★

The primary focus is on communicating information and completing different kinds of real world transactions. Transactional communication is primarily message focused.

⑤ Redundancy ★★★

Spoken language, unlike most written language, has a good deal of redundancy. The next time you're in a conversation, notice the rephrasings, repetitions, elaborations, and little insertions of "I mean" and "you know." Such redundancy helps the hearer to process meaning by offering more time and extra information.

⑥ Reduced Forms (Contraction) ★★

While spoken language does indeed contain a good deal of redundancy, it also has many reduced forms and sentence fragments. Reduction can be phonological ("Djeetyet?" for "Did you eat yet?"), morphological (contractions like "I'll"), syntactic (elliptical forms like "When will you be back?" "Tomorrow, maybe."), or pragmatic (phone rings in a house, child answers and yells to another room in the house, "Mom! Phone!"). These reductions pose significant difficulties, especially for classroom learners who may have initially been exposed to the full forms of the English language.

⑦ Elision ★★

the leaving out of a sound or sounds in speech. For example, speech in English, suppose is often pronounced as [spəʊz], factory as ['fæktri] and mostly as ['məʊsli].

⑧ Liaison ★★

a process in continuous speech which connects the final sound of one word or syllable to the initial sound of the next

(3) Listening Strategies

① Predicting ★★★

This is for generating the learners' schemata. Pre-listening tasks serve to get the learners to think about and talk about the content of what they are about to hear.

② Monitoring ★★★

This is used to confirm predictions made during pre-listening.

③ Listening for Gist ★★

This means understanding the overall message or main idea without focusing on every detail. It helps learners develop global comprehension skills needed for real-world communication.

④ Listening for Specific Information (Scanning) ★★★

When we don't need to understand everything, but only specific parts.

⑤ Listening for Detail ★★

When we cannot afford to ignore anything because we don't know what kind of information we need.

Chapter 05

(4) Listening Activities

① Pictorial Activity **

an activity using pictures or visual materials to activate learners' background knowledge before listening

② Non-pictorial Activity **

an activity that activates learners' schemata before listening without using visual aids, typically through questions, keywords, or discussions

③ Jigsaw Listening ***

In this activity, three different audio clips containing different perspectives are prepared, for example, one containing an interview with someone who has witnessed an accident, one interviewing someone who has seen a UFO, and one about someone who has been involved in a natural catastrophe. Then the class is divided into three groups−Group A, B, and C. Each group goes into a different part of the room and listens to its part of the interview. Each group completes a task (answering comprehension questions, filling in a chart, etc.). Next, new groups are formed, each containing one student from groups A, B, and C. The three students in each new group now report what they heard or role-play the person describing the scene. As a group, the students then decide who the most reliable witness is.

④ Dictogloss ***

This is a type of classroom activity in which learners take notes while listening to a short L2 passage. Learners are subsequently asked to reconstruct the passage. The primary aim of the activity is for learners to notice gaps in their L2 grammar and vocabulary knowledge as they work on the reconstruction.

⑤ Information Transfer 기출 ***

This activity involves getting students to put spoken or written texts into another form, such as a chart, grid, picture, table or diagram−or vice-versa. Make sure that the students can't just copy chunks without understanding them by requiring a different organization to the text. These tasks encourage deep processing of information. The interpretation of text, diagram or tables is a skill that is very useful both in academic and everyday life.

⑥ Partial Dictation 기출 ★★

Partial dictation (PD) is an easier variant of full dictation and a plausible activity in enhancing FL/L2 listening ability. Students are provided with an incomplete written text and fill in missing words while listening to an oral version of the text. Some FL/L2 researchers recommended the use of PD as a reliable, valid, and plausible listening test. Especially, they suggested the use of PD for low-level students when dictation proved too difficult for the students. Using PD helps students focus on missing parts, making it easier for them to follow the text and/or to get its main points.

⑦ Extensive Listening ★★

all types of listening activities that allow learners to receive a lot of comprehensible and enjoyable listening input. These activities can be teacher-directed dictations or read-alouds or self-directed listening for pleasure that can be done outside the classroom. The key consideration here is that learners get to do a lot of meaningful listening practice.

⑧ Intensive Listening ★★★

using taped material. Most course books include tapes and many teachers rely on them to provide their students; with a good listening course. Intensive listening is crucial to help students develop effective listening strategies and build *bottom-up listening skills*, in addition to the *top-down skills* that are emphasized in global listening activities.

(5) Types of Classroom Listening Performance

① Reactive Listening *

This type involves learners listening to the surface structure of an utterance and simply repeating it back, without focusing on deeper meaning. It is often used in pronunciation or choral drills to reinforce sound patterns rather than comprehension.

② Intensive Listening **

Intensive listening focuses on components such as phonemes, words, intonation, or grammatical structures. It aims to help learners notice language details and develop bottom-up skills through focused, controlled listening tasks.

③ Responsive Listening **

Learners listen to short teacher prompts or questions and respond immediately. This type emphasizes quick processing and interaction, involving comprehension checks, clarifications, or simple conversational exchanges.

④ Selective Listening ***

In selective listening, learners listen to longer stretches of discourse to find specific information. The focus is on scanning for key points, such as names, dates, or main ideas, rather than understanding everything globally.

⑤ Extensive Listening **

Extensive listening emphasizes global understanding of longer spoken texts, such as lectures or stories. It aims to develop learners' top-down processing skills and overall comprehension for academic or general purposes.

⑥ Interactive Listening **

Learners participate actively in discussions, debates, or group work that combine listening with speaking and other skills. This type requires learners to process language in real-time and engage in authentic, communicative exchanges.

❸ Reading

(1) Comprehension Process

① Bottom-up Processing 기출 ★★★

Readers must first recognize a multiplicity of linguistic signals (letters, morphemes, syllables, words, phrases, grammatical cues, discourse markers) and use their linguistic data-processing mechanisms to impose some sort of order on these signals. These data-driven operations obviously require a sophisticated knowledge of the language itself.

② Top-down Processing 기출 ★★★

In top-down or conceptually driven processing, we draw on our own intelligence and experience to understand a text.

③ Interactive Processing ★★★

a theory of reading comprehension that sees reading as involving both the accurate and sequential understanding of text based on identification of the meanings of words and sentences in the text as well as the experiences, background information, and predictions that the reader brings to the text

(2) Types of Written Texts

① Simplified Text **

According to Simensen (1987), simplified texts are texts written (1) to illustrate a specific language feature, such as the use of modals or the third-person singular verb form; (2) to modify the amount of new lexical input introduced to learners; or (3) to control for propositional input, or a combination thereof.

② Authentic Text **

Authentic text may be thought of as any text that was written and published for the public. Journal articles, blog posts, and novels are just a few examples. Authentic texts are written for "real world" purposes and audiences: to entertain, inform, explain, guide, document or convince.

③ Authenticity 기출 ***

how closely a text or material resembles real-life language use as it naturally occurs outside the classroom

④ Suitability of Content ***

material that students will find interesting, enjoyable, challenging, and appropriate for their goals in learning English

⑤ Exploitability ***

a text that facilitates the achievement of certain language and content goals, that is exploitable for instructional tasks and techniques, and that is integratable with other skills (listening, speaking, writing)

⑥ Readability ***

a text with lexical aand structural difficulty that will challenge students without overwhelming them

(3) Reading Strategies

① Skimming 기출 ★★★

Skimming is a high-speed reading technique that can save the reader time and help him/her get through a text quickly. The reader skims to get the general sense of a passage, not specific details. When the reader skims, s/he should not read the whole text and eyes should move very quickly over the lines. The reader should read only the parts of the text that will help him/her answer the question.

② Scanning 기출 ★★★

Scanning is a very high-speed reading that the reader does when the reader is looking for a specific piece of information. When s/he scans, the reader has a question in mind and does not read every word, only keywords that will answer the question.

③ Guessing ★★★

When the reader tries to guess the meaning of an unknown word, s/he uses the text surrounding the word—the context—to provide him/her with clues.

④ Inferencing 기출 ★★★

the process of putting pieces of information together so that they make sense is called making an inference. In other words, when the reader "infers" something, s/he is drawing an unstated conclusion from the information that s/he already has.

⑤ Semantic Mapping / Clustering ★★★

It is a strategy of grouping ideas into meaningful clusters. It helps readers provide some order to a long string of ideas or events from a text. The idea of using this tool is to organize the main ideas of the topic they are reading about. This can be done individually, but it is useful as a productive group work technique as students collectively induce order and hierarchy to a passage.

Chapter 05

05

(4) Reading Techniques

① Predicting ★★★

Before starting the text, encourage students to predict what the text will be about based on the title, images, or introductory paragraphs. This technique stimulates curiosity and motivates them to actively engage with the reading to see if their predictions were correct.

② Annotating the Text ★

Teach students to annotate by underlining or highlighting key ideas, new vocabulary, or important information while reading. They can also write short notes or questions in the margins.

③ Summarizing ★

After reading a section, have students summarize the main points in their own words. This ensures that they are actively processing and understanding the material.

④ Questioning ★

Encourage students to ask questions before, during, and after reading. This keeps them actively engaged and allows them to think critically about the text.

⑤ Think-Pair-Share ★

This strategy encourages interaction and engagement. After reading a section, students think about the material, pair up to discuss their thoughts, and then share their ideas with the class.

⑥ Role-playing or Dramatization ★

Have students act out or role-play scenes from the reading material. This makes the reading more engaging and helps them comprehend character motivations and plot developments.

⑦ Post-reading Reflection or Journaling *

After reading, encourage students to reflect on the material by writing in a journal or engaging in a reflection activity. They can express how the text made them feel, what they learned, or any connections they made to their own lives.

⑧ Reciprocal Teaching **

In this technique, students take turns being the "teacher" and guiding the reading discussion. This involves predicting, clarifying, questioning, and summarizing sections of the text.

⑨ Advance Organizer ***

This is to make a general but comprehensive preview of the organizing concept or principle in an anticipated learning activity. It is relevant introductory materials presented in advance in any format of text, graphics, or hypermedia. Instructors may use an advance organizer to present a framework for module content. The aim of this is to relate what a student already knows to the new content to be learned and thus increase retention. Advance organizers should be at a higher level of abstraction, generality, and inclusiveness than the content to be presented.

⑩ Graphic Organizer 기출 ***

This is a pedagogical tool that uses visual symbols to express knowledge and concepts through relationships between them (supplementary tool in while & post activities). This is a specific type of advance organizer and usually applied to listening and reading comprehension pre-task activities.

⑪ Jigsaw Reading 기출 ***

Jigsaw reading is a collaborative reading activity where a text is divided into different sections, and each student (or group) reads only one section. After reading, students come together to share the information from their sections to reconstruct the full meaning of the entire text. This approach promotes interaction, improves comprehension, and develops summarizing and speaking skills.

⑫ Language Experience Approach (LEA) ★★★

The Language Experience Approach (LEA) to teaching reading uses the student's own experiences, vocabulary, and language patterns to create texts for reading instruction and make reading a meaningful process. Students dictate stories to the teacher or orally share a common experience. When written down by or in collaboration with the teacher, these experiences and stories become texts for initial reading instruction. The stories are accessible because they reflect the language and experience of the learners.

⑬ Graded Reader(s) ★★★

A graded reader is an "easy reading" book that supports the extensive reading approach to teaching English as a second or foreign language. Graded readers can be adapted from literacy classics, films, biographies, travel books, etc., or they can be original works written at a less demanding language level. Although they employ simplified language, graded readers do not necessarily lack narrative depth or avoid complex themes; often they cover the same range of "series" themes as books written for native speaker audiences.

⑭ Basal Readers ★★★

Basal readers are textbooks used to teach reading and associated skills to school children. Commonly called "reading books" or "readers" they are usually published as anthologies that combine previously published short stories, excerpts of longer narratives, and original works. A standard basal series comes with individual identical books for students, a Teacher's Edition of the book, and a collection of workbooks, assessments, and activities.

⑮ Extensive Reading 기출 ★★★

For extensive reading, readers spend as much time as possible on reading for pleasure or general language improvement, mostly in real-life situations. Readers choose the text for themselves and tend to read it fast. The materials for extensive reading should be at least 98% comprehensible to the students.

⑯ Sustained Silent Reading ***

A classroom practice where students read self-selected texts silently and independently for an extended, uninterrupted period of time. The main goal is to promote reading fluency, develop a love of reading, and encourage extensive reading habits without teacher interruption or assessment.

⑰ Intensive Reading **

Its goal is to push oneself to build specific skills by taking on difficult material in a focused session.

Apply the Key Terms in Practice

1 Schemata

Read the conversation between two teachers and fill in the blanks with the most appropriate terms.

Ms. Park : I've been thinking about how to improve my students' reading comprehension. They often get stuck on individual words.

Mr. Kim : Right, that sounds like they're relying mostly on ⓐ _____ . processing–decoding words and grammar step by step.

Ms. Park : Exactly. It helps them sometimes, but when the text is long, they lose the overall meaning.

Mr. Kim : That's where ⓑ _____ processing comes in. If they activate their ⓒ _____ , they can predict meaning and fill in gaps even if they don't know every word.

Ms. Park : True. For example, when we read a passage about online shopping, I tried to build their ⓓ _____ schemata first by asking about their own experiences buying things online. That gave them a frame of reference.

Mr. Kim : Nice. And for ⓔ _____ schemata, we can guide them on how the text is structured. Like showing them how news articles usually start with the main point, or how narratives follow a sequence.

Ms. Park : Yes, that way they're not just decoding vocabulary, but using expectations about the genre to support comprehension.

Mr. Kim : I've also noticed that when I combine both approaches, it works best. I'll do a quick pre-reading activity to activate ⓑ _____ knowledge, then during reading, I give them short exercises to practice ⓐ _____ skills like recognizing signal words or verb forms.

Ms. Park : That makes sense. So students learn to adjust their processing approach, depending on the task.

Mr. Kim : Exactly. The balance is important. Too much ⓐ _____, and they drown in details. Too much ⓑ _____, and they guess wildly without checking the text.

Ms. Park : I like that. Maybe I'll design my next lesson around both–start with a schema-activation discussion, then move into some close reading tasks.

Mr. Kim : Perfect. That way we're training their receptive skills more effectively.

❷ Comprehension Level

Read the passage and follow the directions.

🔹 **Reading Text**

"In 2023, the city government launched a new recycling campaign to reduce plastic waste. The campaign introduced stricter waste-separation rules, gave incentives to eco-friendly businesses, and ran educational programs for citizens. Within one year, plastic use dropped by 40%, and many households improved their recycling habits. (*omitted*) However, experts warn that recycling alone is not enough and stress the need for lifestyle changes, such as reducing single-use plastics and choosing reusable products."

After reading a short passage about climate change, Ms. Park talks with her students to check their comprehension at different levels.

Ms. Park : Alright, everyone, let's check how well you understood the passage. Minji, when did the city launch the new recycling campaign?

Minji : It started in 2023.

Ms. Park : Good. Now, Jihun, can you find how many different actions the campaign included?

Jihun : There are three actions mentioned: stricter waste-separation rules, incentives to eco-friendly businesses, and educational programs for citizens.

Ms. Park : Exactly. Now, Soyeon, based on what the passage says, what can we understand about the relationship between recycling and lifestyle changes?

Soyeon : I think recycling helps, but it's not enough on its own. People also need to change their daily habits, like using fewer single-use products, if we really want to make a big difference.

Ms. Park : That's an interesting point. Daehyun, do you agree with the expert's opinion that lifestyle changes are necessary? Why or why not?

Daehyun : Yes, I agree. Even if we recycle, plastic production is still increasing. Without changing people's habits, the problem won't be solved.

Ms. Park : Nicely reasoned. Finally, Sumin, after reading this passage, how has it influences the way you think about your own life and choices?

Sumin : Yes, it made me realize that I should reduce my plastic use and avoid single-use products. I also feel more responsible for helping the environment.

Ms. Park : That's exactly what I hoped you'd take away. Understanding the facts is important, but connecting them to your own actions matters just as much.

Based on the conversation above, complete the table below.

Level	Focus	Teacher's Question
ⓐ _____	Understanding directly stated facts	ⓕ _____ _____
ⓑ _____	Integrating details from different part of the text	ⓖ _____ _____
ⓒ _____	Making logical assumptions based on the passage	ⓗ _____ _____
ⓓ _____	Evaluating ideas or arguments	ⓘ _____ _____
ⓔ _____	Responding personally and emotionally	ⓙ _____ _____

Chapter 05

③ Types of Spoken Language

Read the passages and fill in the blanks with the most appropriate terms.

Below are a listening script excerpted from today's listening lesson and its comments.

▢ Listening Script

Setting: *A customer, Mina, visits a travel agency to book a vacation package.*

Staff : Good afternoon! How can I help you today?

Mina : Hi, I'd like to book a family vacation for next month. Do you have any recommendations?

Staff : Sure! We have a 5-day package to Jeju Island. It includes flights, hotel, and a guided tour.

Mina : That sounds great. How much is it?

Staff : The total cost is 850,000 won per person.

Mina : Okay, and can I pay in installments?

Staff : Yes, we offer a three-month installment plan. Would you like me to reserve it for you?

Mina : Yes, please! That would be perfect.

(ellipsis)

🔗 Comments

After listening to the given dialogue, students complete a True/False activity to check comprehension of specific details. These questions require students to pay attention to exchanging factual information, such as booking details, prices, and payment options, which are typical features of ⓐ _____ dialogues.

In contrast, ⓑ _____ dialogues focus more on maintaining personal relationships and social connections. They often include greetings, small talk, and sharing personal experiences rather than exchanging detailed information. Recognizing the differences between these two types of dialogues helps students better understand the purpose and structure of conversations.

4 Characteristics of Spoken Language

Read the conversation between two teachers during the classroom meeting, and fill in the blanks with the most appropriate terms.

💬 Classroom Meeting: Ms. Park & Mr. Yoo

Ms. Park : I've noticed that many of my students can read fairly well, but when it comes to listening, they often get lost. I think part of the problem is that spoken English is so different from written English.

Mr. Yoo : Absolutely. Features like ⓐ _____ and ⓑ _____ make it difficult. For example, in natural speech, "next day" often sounds like *nexday*, and "want to" becomes *wanna*. Students don't realize they're hearing familiar words because parts are dropped or linked together.

Ms. Park : Exactly. Sometimes they say, "Teacher, that word wasn't in the recording!" when in fact it was–just reduced. I think we should design listening tasks that raise awareness of these reductions.

Mr. Yoo : One idea is to give them short dialogues and ask them to mark where ⓐ _____ or ⓑ _____ happens. For instance, listen to "Did you eat?" and notice how it often sounds like "Jeet?"

Ms. Park : That's good. I also want to address ⓒ _____ in spoken language. Students expect every word to be essential, but in conversation, we repeat ourselves, add fillers like *you know* or *well*, and use ⓒ _____ to give listeners more time to process.

Mr. Yoo : True. We can show them how ⓒ _____ actually helps comprehension instead of confusing them. Maybe we could play a short clip, then ask students to underline repeated words and fillers, and discuss why speakers use them.

Ms. Park : Yes, and that could help lower their anxiety. If they understand that not every word carries new meaning, they can focus on the key message.

Mr. Yoo　：Agreed. So, for our next lesson cycle, let's include three components:

* ⓐ _____ **and** ⓑ _____ **awareness activities** with short
  listening drills
* **dictation practice** where students notice reduced forms
* ⓒ _____ **analysis** in authentic conversations, showing how repetition
  aids comprehension

Ms. Park：Perfect. That way, students develop both ⓓ _____ **listening**
　　　　　skills–recognizing sounds–and ⓔ _____ **listening skills**–
　　　　　using redundancy and context to fill in gaps.

⑤ Listening Strategies

Read the listening script and listening worksheet below and follow the directions.

> 📦 Listening Script
>
> Anna : Hey, Ben! Do you want to do something fun this weekend?
>
> Ben : Sure! I was thinking of going hiking on Saturday morning.
>
> Anna : That sounds great. Where do you want to go?
>
> Ben : I found a nice place called Maple Hill. It's not too far from the city.
>
> Anna : Perfect! Let's meet at the subway station then. What time?
>
> Ben : How about 9 a.m.? We can have lunch there after hiking.
>
> Anna : Sounds good. But wait… did you check the weather?
>
> Ben : Yeah… they said it might rain in the afternoon.
>
> Anna : Oh no. If it rains, what will you do?
>
> Ben : I'll probably visit my grandmother instead. She asked me to come on Sunday, but I can switch if the weather's bad.
>
> Anna : Okay, so the plan is: hiking Saturday morning at 9 a.m., and if it rains, you'll visit your grandma.
>
> Ben : Exactly. Let's hope for good weather!

📦 While Listening Worksheet

Task 1. First Listening

Listen to the conversation once and choose the best answer.

Q. What are the two friends mainly talking about?

  a) A movie they watched last week

  b) Their weekend plans

  c) A problems at school

Task 2. Second Listening

Listen again and write the missing information.

Q1. Where is Ben going on Saturday morning?

_____

Q2. What time will they meet at the subway station?

_____

Task 3. Third Listening

Listen carefully and answer the following questions.

Q1. Why might Ben visit his grandmother earlier than planned?

_____

Q2. What problem could they have with their Saturday plan?

_____

Task 4. Thinking Beyond the Words

Listen again to this part: "they said it might rain in the afternoon."

Q. What can you guess about Ben's feelings?

   a) He's worried because their hiking plan might be affected.
   b) He's frustrated because changing plans is inconvenient for him.
   c) He feels relieved because he prefers visiting his grandmother instead.

Chapter 05

Based on the passage above, identify the listening strategy that is the most appropriate to complete each task successfully.

Task 1 – ⓐ _____
Task 2 – ⓑ _____
Task 3 – ⓒ _____
Task 4 – ⓓ _____

⑥ Listening Activity

Read the conversation between two teachers and fill in the blanks with the most appropriate terms.

The following is a natural conversation between Ms. Yoo and Mr. Choi, highlighting the problem of word-level listening and how ⓐ _____ can help.

Mr. Choi : Ms. Yoo, I'm worried about my students' listening skills. They can pick out single words, but they really struggle to understand sentences or longer passages.

Ms. Yoo : Ah, that's a common issue. It sounds like they're stuck at the word-recognition level and can't yet process language in chunks.

Mr. Choi : Exactly. They focus on catching each word, and by the time they do, they've already missed the rest of the sentence.

Ms. Yoo : In that case, I'd recommend trying a(n) ⓐ _____ activity.

Mr. Choi : ⓐ _____? How would that help?

Ms. Yoo : It's very effective because it trains students to listen for meaning and structure, not just isolated words. Here's how it works: You read a short passage at normal speed–maybe two or three times. Students take notes, but they can't write everything word-for-word. Afterward, they work together in pairs or groups to reconstruct the passage as accurately as possible.

Mr. Choi : So instead of writing every single word, they're piecing the text together from memory?

Ms. Yoo : Exactly. That pushes them to pay attention to grammar, collocations, and overall meaning rather than obsessing over individual words. It also engages both ⓑ _____ processing–using context and background knowledge–and ⓒ _____ processing–decoding sounds into words.

Mr. Choi : I see. That sounds like it could shift their focus from word-level listening to understanding whole sentences.

Ms. Yoo : Yes, and the group work is key. When students compare notes, they fill in each other's gaps, so even weaker listeners benefit from peer support. Over time, this helps them build stronger listening comprehension skills.

Mr. Choi : That makes sense. I'll try ⓐ _____ with them next week. Thanks for the suggestion!

Ms. Yoo : Anytime. Let me know how it goes–I'm sure they'll find it challenging but rewarding.

7 Reading Strategies (1)

Read the passage and the comprehension questions below, and identify the most appropriate reading strategy to answer each question.

Reading Text

Last summer, the city library launched its "Read for Change" campaign to encourage eco-friendly reading habits. As part of the campaign, they introduced a digital lending system, organized weekly book-sharing events, and offered rewards to readers who reused old books. According to a survey, 2,500 people participated in the events, and over 15,000 e-books were borrowed during the campaign. *(omitted)*

However, library staff reported a challenge: many participants still preferred printed books despite the convenience of digital lending. Experts suggested that more interactive digital features might encourage readers to fully shift to e-books in the future.

Q1. What is the main purpose of the "Read for Change" campaign?

    a) To reduce printed books
    b) To promote eco-friendly reading habits
    c) To increase library visitors
    d) To support local bookstores

Q2. According to the text, how many e-books were borrowed during the campaign?

    a) 2,500
    b) 7,500
    c) 15,000
    d) 20,000

Q3. Even though the library introduced a digital lending system, many participants still preferred printed books. What could be a possible reason for this preference?

a) Printed books are more expensive.

b) Printed books provide a different reading experience.

c) Participants didn't know how to borrow e-books.

d) The library limited the number of e-books.

Question 1 − ⓐ _____

Question 2 − ⓑ _____

Question 3 − ⓒ _____

Chapter 05

8 Reading Strategies (2)

Read the conversation between Hyejin and Dana, and identify TWO reading strategies that Dana recommended.

Hyejin : Ugh, this article is so hard to understand. There's so much information, and I keep losing track of what the author is trying to say.

Dana : I know what you mean. When that happens to me, I try to picture the situation in my head as I read. I focus on the key ideas and imagine what's happening based on the sentences. It helps me follow the flow of the text more easily.

Hyejin : Oh, so I can create a picture in my mind about what's going on to understand it better?

Dana : Exactly! And here's another tip–you don't always need to read the entire article carefully. If the question only asks about the author's opinion, you can focus on the parts where the author shares ideas or arguments. That way, you won't waste time on sections you don't need.

Hyejin : That actually makes sense. I'll try both strategies next time.

9 Reading Activity (1)

Read the conversation between two teachers and fill in each blank with the most appropriate term.

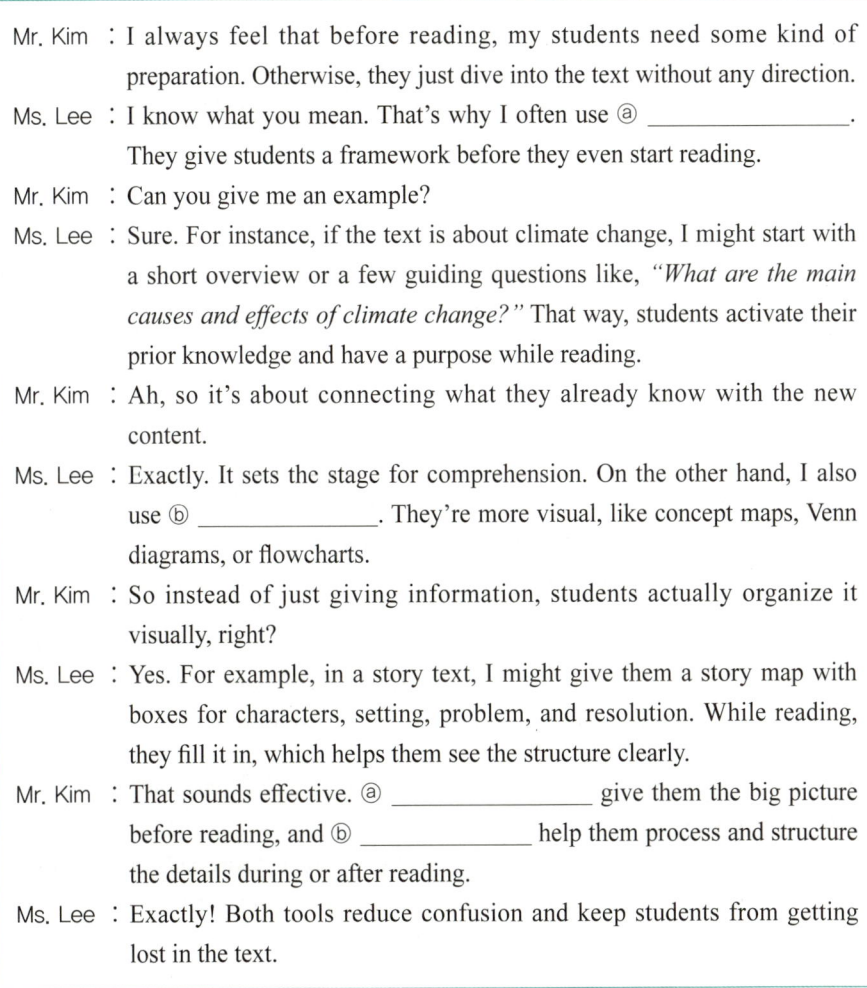

Mr. Kim : I always feel that before reading, my students need some kind of preparation. Otherwise, they just dive into the text without any direction.

Ms. Lee : I know what you mean. That's why I often use ⓐ _____.
They give students a framework before they even start reading.

Mr. Kim : Can you give me an example?

Ms. Lee : Sure. For instance, if the text is about climate change, I might start with a short overview or a few guiding questions like, *"What are the main causes and effects of climate change?"* That way, students activate their prior knowledge and have a purpose while reading.

Mr. Kim : Ah, so it's about connecting what they already know with the new content.

Ms. Lee : Exactly. It sets the stage for comprehension. On the other hand, I also use ⓑ _____. They're more visual, like concept maps, Venn diagrams, or flowcharts.

Mr. Kim : So instead of just giving information, students actually organize it visually, right?

Ms. Lee : Yes. For example, in a story text, I might give them a story map with boxes for characters, setting, problem, and resolution. While reading, they fill it in, which helps them see the structure clearly.

Mr. Kim : That sounds effective. ⓐ _____ give them the big picture before reading, and ⓑ _____ help them process and structure the details during or after reading.

Ms. Lee : Exactly! Both tools reduce confusion and keep students from getting lost in the text.

⑩ Reading Activity (2)

Read the classroom dialogue below and identify the teaching approach being used.

Ms. Yoo and students co-create reading materials using the _____. She acts as a scribe, turning students' spoken words into a shared text.

Teacher (Ms. Yoo) ： Good morning, everyone. Today, we're going to make our own story together. Let's think about something we all experienced. What did we do last Friday?

Minho ： We went to the science museum!

Teacher ： Yes, that's right. What did we see there?

Sumin ： We saw the dinosaur skeletons.

Teacher ： *(writing on the board as she repeats aloud)* "We saw the dinosaur skeletons." Great sentence, Sumin.

Jiwon ： We also watched a space movie in the planetarium.

Teacher ： *(adding to the text, pointing as she reads aloud)* Perfect. "We also watched a space movie in the planetarium."

Hana ： The chairs moved! It felt like we were flying.

Teacher ： *(writing it down, showing the class the text)* Nice detail, Hana. "The chairs moved, and it felt like we were flying."

Ms. Yoo continues writing as students take turns contributing. She points at each sentence so students see how their spoken words become written text.

Teacher ： Is there anything to add? Minho, how did you feel about the trip?

Minho ： It was really exciting!

Teacher ： *(writing on the board)* "It was really exciting!" Okay, let's read what we have together. Follow along with your eyes as we read.

Students and teacher read aloud in chorus, pointing to the sentences.

"We went to the science museum. We saw the dinosaur skeletons. We also watched a space movie in the planetarium. The chairs moved, and it felt like we were flying. It was really exciting!"

Teacher : Wonderful job! This is our story. How about adding some pictures to go with it, so we can make our own class book? That way, we'll have our own storybook to read again and again.

⑪ Intensive Reading and Extensive Reading

After reading the teacher's reflection fill in the blanks.

🗍 Teacher's Reflection

This week, I tried two different approaches to reading in my classroom.

For ⓐ _____ reading, I relied on ⓑ _____, structured textbooks that use controlled vocabulary and targeted grammar points to guide students step by step. In these lessons, we carefully examined short passages together, breaking them down to look at key vocabulary, sentence patterns, and grammar structures. I found this approach effective in helping students develop accuracy and notice details they often overlook–for example, how connectors create relationships between ideas. That said, the process was quite teacher-led and required a slower pace, so a few students struggled to stay focused and sometimes lost interest.

In contrast, ⓒ _____ reading took a very different form. I introduced a variety of ⓓ _____–books written with simplified grammar and controlled vocabulary that cater to different proficiency levels–and gave students the freedom to choose what they wanted to read. Unlike the more structured intensive lessons, this activity allowed students to read at their own pace and enjoy the stories without worrying about understanding every single word. Several students even mentioned that they felt more confident because they could follow the narratives smoothly. I also noticed lively class discussions afterward, where many were eager to share their favorite parts and personal opinions. Through this approach, I saw clear gains in reading fluency, motivation, and learner autonomy.

Looking back, I realized that ⓐ _____ reading is most effective for building accuracy and form-awareness, whereas ⓒ _____ reading better suited for improving fluency, motivation, and confidence. In the future, I hope to combine the strengths of both approaches to create a more balanced and engaging reading program for my students.

Answers

1 Schemata

ⓐ bottom-up
ⓑ top-down
ⓒ schemata
ⓓ content
ⓔ formal

2 Comprehension Level

ⓐ Literal
ⓑ Reorganization
ⓒ Inferential
ⓓ Critical
ⓔ Appreciative
ⓕ when did the city launch the new recycling campaign?
ⓖ can you find how many different actions the campaign included?
ⓗ what can we understand about the relationship between recycling and lifestyle changes?
ⓘ do you agree with the expert's opinion that lifestyle changes are necessary? Why or why not?
ⓙ how has it influences the way you think about your own life and choices?

3 Types of Spoken Language

ⓐ transactional/informational
ⓑ interpersonal/interactional

4 Characteristics of Spoken Language

ⓐ elision
ⓑ liaison
ⓒ redundancy
ⓓ bottom-up
ⓔ top-down

5 Listening Strategies

ⓐ Listening for gist/global understanding
ⓑ Listening for specific information (scanning)
ⓒ Listening for detail
ⓓ Inferential listening

6 Listening Activity

ⓐ dictogloss / Dictogloss
ⓑ top-down
ⓒ bottom-up

7 Reading Strategies (1)

ⓐ Skimming
ⓑ Scanning
ⓒ Inferencing

8 Reading Strategies (2)

Visualizing, Selective Reading

9 Reading Activity (1)

ⓐ advance organizers / Advance organizers
ⓑ graphic organizers

10 Reading Activity (2)

Language Experience Approach

11 Intensive Reading and Extensive Reading

ⓐ intensive
ⓑ basal readers
ⓒ extensive
ⓓ graded readers

Productive Skills

Map the Key Terms

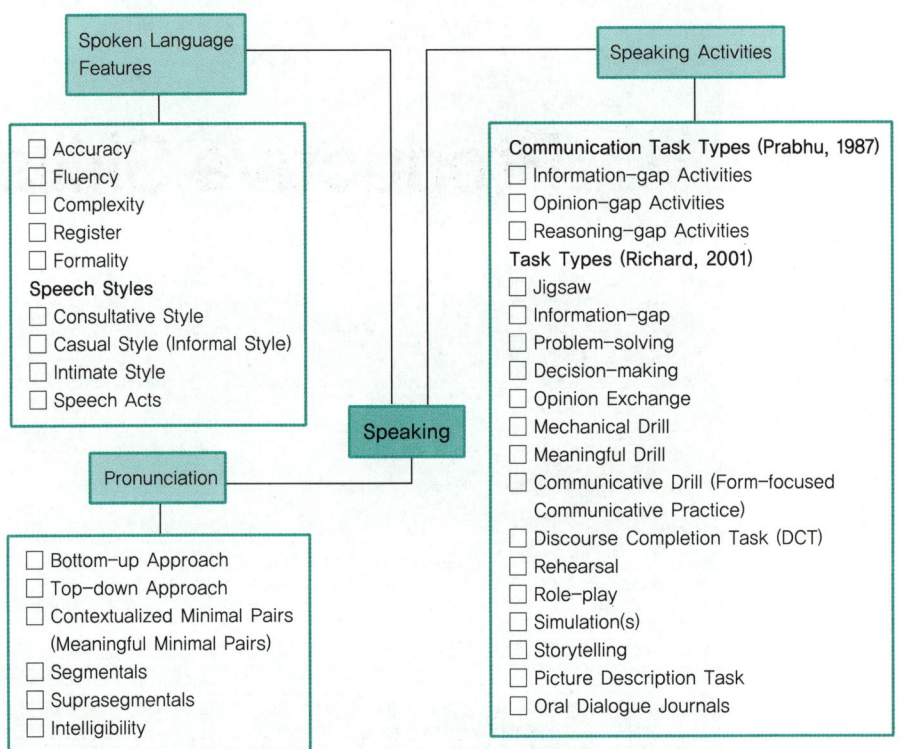

Spoken Language Features

- ☐ Accuracy
- ☐ Fluency
- ☐ Complexity
- ☐ Register
- ☐ Formality

Speech Styles
- ☐ Consultative Style
- ☐ Casual Style (Informal Style)
- ☐ Intimate Style
- ☐ Speech Acts

Pronunciation

- ☐ Bottom–up Approach
- ☐ Top–down Approach
- ☐ Contextualized Minimal Pairs (Meaningful Minimal Pairs)
- ☐ Segmentals
- ☐ Suprasegmentals
- ☐ Intelligibility

Speaking

Speaking Activities

Communication Task Types (Prabhu, 1987)
- ☐ Information–gap Activities
- ☐ Opinion–gap Activities
- ☐ Reasoning–gap Activities

Task Types (Richard, 2001)
- ☐ Jigsaw
- ☐ Information–gap
- ☐ Problem–solving
- ☐ Decision–making
- ☐ Opinion Exchange
- ☐ Mechanical Drill
- ☐ Meaningful Drill
- ☐ Communicative Drill (Form–focused Communicative Practice)
- ☐ Discourse Completion Task (DCT)
- ☐ Rehearsal
- ☐ Role–play
- ☐ Simulation(s)
- ☐ Storytelling
- ☐ Picture Description Task
- ☐ Oral Dialogue Journals

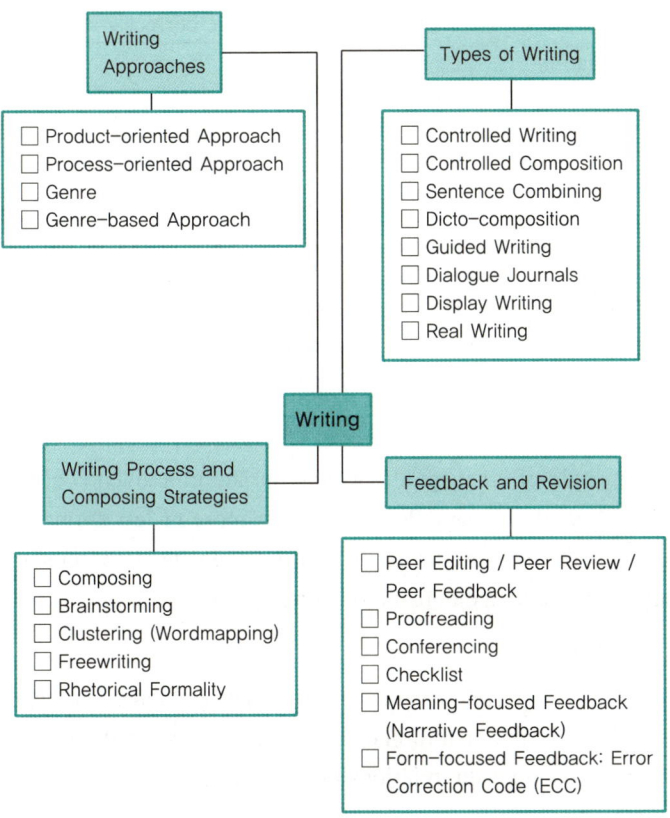

Writing Approaches
- ☐ Product–oriented Approach
- ☐ Process–oriented Approach
- ☐ Genre
- ☐ Genre–based Approach

Types of Writing
- ☐ Controlled Writing
- ☐ Controlled Composition
- ☐ Sentence Combining
- ☐ Dicto–composition
- ☐ Guided Writing
- ☐ Dialogue Journals
- ☐ Display Writing
- ☐ Real Writing

Writing

Writing Process and Composing Strategies
- ☐ Composing
- ☐ Brainstorming
- ☐ Clustering (Wordmapping)
- ☐ Freewriting
- ☐ Rhetorical Formality

Feedback and Revision
- ☐ Peer Editing / Peer Review / Peer Feedback
- ☐ Proofreading
- ☐ Conferencing
- ☐ Checklist
- ☐ Meaning–focused Feedback (Narrative Feedback)
- ☐ Form–focused Feedback: Error Correction Code (ECC)

02 Master the Key Terms

❶ Speaking

(1) Spoken Language Features

① Accuracy **

It means that the speakers are required to use the correct vocabulary, grammar, and pronunciation.

② Fluency ***

In terms of speaking skills, it means that the speakers are required to be able to keep going when speaking spontaneously. It is the unfettered flow of language production or comprehension usually without focal attention on language forms.

③ Complexity **

a composite measure of language use, normally reflecting the length of utterances and the amount of subordination used

④ Register ***

This is the style of language that is appropriate in a given context. Thus, the different types of language that are used in more or less formal contexts are examples of different registers. In addition, register may refer to specialist language that is used in different professions or hobbies.

⑤ Formality 기출 ***

This refers to the degree of conventionality and politeness in language use. It indicates how formal or informal the language is, depending on factors such as the social context, the relationship between speakers, and the purpose of communication.

⑥ Speech Styles **

- Consultative Style: It's a style characterized by a semi-formal vocabulary, often unplanned and reliant on the listener's responses and overall participation.
- Casual Style (Informal Style): As the name says, this style is characterized by its casuality, with a flexible and informal vocabulary that may include slang. It's usually unplanned, pretty relaxed, and reliant on the fluid back and forth between those involved, without any particular order.
- Intimate Style: This is the speech style that's reserved for people who have a really close connection. It's casual and relaxed and goes beyond words, as it incorporates nonverbal communication and even personal language codes, such as terms of endearment and expressions whose meaning is only understood by the participants, besides slang.

⑦ Speech Acts 기출 ***

one of the abilities enabling social interaction, using appropriate forms to accomplish such purposes as requesting, answering, greeting, agreeing, disagreeing, etc.

- Locutionary Meaning: the basic literal or propositional meaning of an utterance (or written text) that is conveyed by its words and structures
- Illocutionary Force: the intended effect that an utterance or text has on the hearer or reader
- Perlocutionary Force: the actual effect the utterance has on the hearer

Chapter 06

(2) Speaking Activities

① Communication Task Types (Prabhu, 1987) ★★★

- Information-gap Activities: These involve the transfer of information from one person to another, from one form to another or from one place to another. For example, two students might have different schedules, but they want to find time to get together to have tea. They need to get relevant information from each other to determine when they are both free, as well as when the available times coincide with when a tea house is open. This type of activity allows students to request information, ask for clarification and negotiate both meaning, particularly when misunderstandings occur, and appropriate conclusions to the task.

- Opinion-gap Activities: activities that ask students to convey their own personal preferences, feelings or ideas about a particular situation. On a higher level, you might ask them to take part in a discussion or debate about a political or local issue. On a lower level, you might ask them to complete a story. In these types of activities, there is no right or wrong answer, and, therefore, there is no objective means by which to judge outcomes, outside of whether what the students do or say addresses the task at hand. You might require them to speak or write for a certain amount (words or time) and you might ask them to use certain constructions.

- Reasoning-gap Activities: activities in which you ask your students to derive some information from that which you give them. They are required to comprehend and convey information, much as in an information gap activity, but the information that they are asked to convey is not exactly the same that they comprehend. They are asked to use reason and logic to decide what information to convey and what resolution to make for the problem at hand. For example, you might ask your students to make a decision between speed and cost or cost and quality, given a certain situation and various constraints.

② Task Types (Richard, 2001) 기출 ★★★

- Jigsaw: a communicative activity in which two or more interlocutors have differing pieces of information that must be combined in order to complete successfully the activity. For example, learners may be given different components of a character's daily activities, with the goal of the task being for the learners to recreate the character's routine. Learners must share their information in order to complete the entire routine. The jigsaw task is identified following characteristics:

(a) Each interactant holds a different portion of information which must be exchanged and manipulated in order to reach the task outcome.

(b) Both interactants are required to request and supply this information to each other.

(c) Interactants have the same or convergent goals.

(d) Only one acceptable outcome is possible from their attempts to meet this goal.

As jigsaw task interactants, X and Y hold dual roles as information holders, suppliers, and requesters, each having a piece of the 'puzzle' which must be joined together. The task participants are expected to achieve a convergent goal and a single outcome which allow no options, in order to complete the task. Thus, Pica claims that "this task can be considered the type of task most likely to generate opportunities for interactants to work toward comprehension, feedback, and interlanguage modification processes related to successful SLA".

• Information-gap: pedagogical tasks in which different learners each have part of the information required to complete the task, usually to solve a problem or make a decision. (Simply put, task requires that one person describes a picture and the other person draws the picture.) For example, learners may be asked to find a lost friend and each be given different information about him, such as the country where he is or the type of work he does. To find the person, the learners have to exchange the information that they have. An information gap task is defined as one participant holding information that the other does not already know, but needs to know in order to complete a task. The gap in the distribution of information results in a one-way flow of information from the sending one interactant (X) to the receiving interactant (Y). Thus, interactants have less of a chance to modify production toward greater comprehensibility since the task assigns each interactant a fixed role. Although the "information gap" task limits interlanguage modification, the activity has been even more widely used than the jigsaw in language teaching and learning, particularly in characterizing activities which motivate communication among classroom language learners.

• Problem-solving: A problem-solving task is characterized as a task oriented toward a single resolution of outcome. In this task, information is expected to flow two ways, but participation of all students is not necessary for successful completion of the exercise.

- Decision-making: A decision-making task has a number of possible outcomes available to participants in contrast to the problem-solving task. The decision-making participants can choose to seek, withhold, or exchange information and reach one of many possible decisions as they work to complete this task. Such discussion tasks are open-ended and do not require the participation of all students. There is also no expectation of convergence of opinions to any particular outcome.
- Opinion Exchange: The opinion exchange task, which engages learners in discussion and exchange of ideas is also not expected to converge toward a single goal, but any number of outcome options, including no outcome at all, is possible for participants. To complete the task, interaction is possible but not required by the participant and even a single interactant might dominate. Moral, ethical, religious, and political issues are often sensitive, "hot" topics for classroom debates, arguments, and discussions. Students can get involved in the content-centered nature of such activity and thus pave the way for automatic processing of language itself. Here are a few such issues: woman's right, privacy rights and government "snooping", euthanasia, environmental crises, etc.

③ Mechanical Drill **

techniques that require only one correct response from a student without connection with reality

④ Meaningful Drill **

What some have called meaningful drills can add some reality, but may stretch the concept of drill too far. And the process may continue on as the teacher reinforces certain grammatical or phonological elements, but connects utterances to reality. This is more appropriately a case of what one could call meaningful practice, useful in virtually any communicative classroom.

⑤ Communicative Drill (Form-focused Communicative Practice) **

A communicative drill is one in which the type of response is controlled but the student provides his or her own content or information. A further extension of meaningful communicative practice is found in form-focused communicative practice.

⑥ Discourse Completion Task (DCT) *

This is a data collection instrument that is often used in research on pragmatics. Learners are provided with a scenario in which they must use language to perform some type of action, such as making a request or declining an invitation. Sometimes learners are also provided with an initial utterance to get them started. Then learners are asked to write (or less often, speak) what they would say in the specific context to accomplish the purpose stated in the task.

⑦ Rehearsal **

This is the act of practicing or repeating an utterance or task before producing it. Rehearsal can take place internally in the learner's mind or it can be done verbally.

⑧ Role-play **

Students pretend they are in various social contexts and have a variety of social roles. In role-play activities, the teacher gives information to the learners such as who they are and what they think or feel. Thus, the teacher can tell the student that "you are David, you go to the doctor and tell him what happened last night and..."

⑨ Simulation(s) **

These are very similar to role-plays but this is more elaborate. Students can bring items to the class to create a realistic environment. For instance, if a student is acting as a singer, she brings a microphone to sing and so on.

⑩ Storytelling *

Students can briefly summarize a tale or story they heard from somebody beforehand, or they may create their own stories to tell their classmates. It fosters creative thinking.

⑪ Picture Description Task *

This is a communicative activity that can be used to elicit L2 production. Learners are given a series of pictures that they must describe. Sometimes the pictures are unrelated to each other and are to be described individually. Other times, learners must use the pictures to create a narrative, based either on the order of pictures provided for them or by putting the pictures into a logical order themselves. Learners can perform these tasks either by themselves or with other learners in an information gap task.

⑫ Oral Dialogue Journals *

Students create audio recordings of thoughts, reactions, questions, and concerns that the teacher can listen to and respond to.

(3) Pronunciation

① Bottom-up Approach **

This approach begins with the articulation of individual sounds and works up towards intonation, stress and rhythm. In the bottom-up approach, the basic idea is that if you teach the segments, the suprasegmental features will take care of by themselves.

② Top-down Approach **

This approach begins with patterns of intonation and brings separate sounds into sharper focus as and when required. In the top-down approach, the assumption is that once the prosodic features are in place, the necessary segmental discriminations will follow accordingly.

③ Contextualized Minimal Pairs (Meaningful Minimal Pairs) ***

pairs of words that differ by only one sound, embedded in meaningful or contextualized situation. They are designed to help learners perceive and produce subtle phonological differences through communicative or semi-communicative tasks.

④ Segmentals **

Segmentals consist of the phonemes of the language, or its smallest meaningful units.

⑤ Suprasegmentals **

Suprasegmentals include intonation, rhythm, and stress. These features can have an even greater impact on intelligibility than the mispronunciation of sounds.

⑥ Intelligibility ***

how clearly a person speaks so that his/her speech is comprehensible to a listener

② Writing

(1) Writing Approaches

① **Product-oriented Approach** ★★

The product-oriented approach to the teaching of writing emphasizes mechanical aspects of writing, such as focusing on grammatical and syntactical structures and imitating models. This approach is primarily concerned with "correctness" and form of the final product.

② **Process-oriented Approach** ★★★

The process-oriented approach emphasizes that writing itself is a developmental process that creates self-discovery and meaning. While the mechanical aspects of writing are important, they should not interfere with the composing process. This composing process requires much revision and rewriting. The teacher intervenes and guides students during the composing process but initially does not emphasize "correctness" and the final product; the emphasis on "correctness" and the final product comes only toward the very end of the writing process. Instead of worrying about form, students concentrate on conveying a written message.

③ **Genre** ★★

a type of discourse that occurs in a particular setting, that has distinctive and recognizable patterns and norms of organization and structure, and that has particular and distinctive communicative functions. For example: business reports, news broadcasts, speeches, letters, advertisements, etc. In constructing texts, the writer must employ certain features conventionally associated with texts from the genre in which he or she is writing. In reading a text the reader similarly anticipates certain features of the text based on genre expectations.

06

④ Genre-based Approach *******

The genre approach to the teaching of writing is mainly concerned, as the name indicates, with teaching particular genres that students need control of in order to succeed in particular situations. This might include an emphasis on the content of the text as well as the context in which the text is produced. The fundamental principle that underlies the genre approach is that language is functional; that is, it is through language that we achieve certain goals. Three essential features of the general;

(a) the context, which includes the situation and audience

(b) the content, which indicates the information and message conveyed

(c) the construction, that is, how the texts of the genre are typically constructed in terms of the layout and language

(2) Writing Process and Composing Strategies

① Composing ******

the thinking, drafting, and revising procedures involved in planned writing

② Brainstorming *******

This is a form of prewriting in which a student or group of students write down as many thoughts as possible on a topic without paying attention to organization, sentence structure or spelling. Brainstorming serves to gather ideas, viewpoints, or ideas related to a writing topic and is said to help the writer produce ideas.

③ Clustering (Wordmapping) ******

Clustering begins with a key word or central idea placed in the center of a page around which the student jots down in a few minutes all of the free associations triggered by the subject matter. The words or phrases generated are put on the page or board in a pattern which takes shapes from the connections the writer sees as each new thought emerges.

④ Freewriting ******

writing simply to start the "flow" of writing, with little thought to grammaticality, spelling, logical thinking, or organization

⑤ Rhetorical Formality *

organizational conventions in writing for connecting sentences, showing relationships, opening paragraphs, using subordination, and so on, that extend beyond the sentence level

(3) Types of Writing

① Controlled Writing **

Controlled writing takes place when learners are supplied with "a great deal of the content and/or form [such as] an outline to complete, a paragraph to manipulate, a model to follow, or a passage to continue." Controlled writing assists in both preventing errors that apparently occur from first language interference and reinforcing proper use of second language patterns. Therefore, engaging learners in controlled writing in L2 can be "as an exercise in habit formation (in which the EFL/ESL learner) is simply a manipulator of previously learned language structured."

② Controlled Composition **

Controlled composition focuses the students' attention on specific features of the written language. It is a good method of reinforcing grammar, vocabulary, and syntax in context. Students can be aware of the conventions of written English such as identification, punctuation, connecting words, and spelling.

③ Sentence Combining **

Combining sentences encourages a writer to take two or more short, choppy sentences and combine them into one effective sentence. By learning this skill, students enhance their writing style. Sentence combining skill is something that will develop over several short practice sessions and should be considered as one component of an overall writing program.

④ Dicto-composition ***

A paragraph is read at normal speed, usually two or three times; then the teacher asks students to re-write the paragraph to the best of their recollection of the reading. In one of several variations of the dicto-comp techniques, the teacher, after reading the passage, puts key words from the paragraph, in sequence, on the chalkboard as cues for the students.

⑤ Guided Writing 기출 **

Guided writing is an extension of controlled writing. It is less controlled than the controlled writing in that it gives students some but not all of the content and form of the sentences they will use. Their finished products will be similar but not exactly alike. Students are given a first or last sentence, an outline to fill out, a series of questions to respond to, or information to include in their piece of writing.

⑥ Dialogue Journals ***

Dialogue journals are written conversations in which a learner and teacher (or another writing partner) communicate regularly (daily, weekly, or on a schedule that fits the educational setting) over a semester, school year, or course. Learners write as much as they choose on a wide range of topics and in a variety of genres and styles. The teacher writes back regularly, responding to questions and comments, introducing new topics, or asking questions.

⑦ Display Writing **

primarily for the display of a student's knowledge

⑧ Real Writing **

The reader does not know the answer (to a question or problem) and genuinely wants information. Peer-editing provides real writing opportunity, as do various forms of informal writing like diaries, letters, postcards, notes, and personal messages.

(4) Feedback and Revision

① Peer Editing / Peer Review / Peer Feedback 기출 ***

Editing a peer's piece of writing is called peer-editing. Some students may see peer-editing as unbeneficial to learning and may prefer teachers to do all the editing. Peer-editing allows students to identify each other's strengths and weaknesses in their writing skills while being less reliant on the teacher. When students experience peer-editing, they become more empowered, and more objective in their writing.

② Proofreading **

After you (the student) have rewritten your paper, go over it carefully to see if the language sounds correct and if your message seems complete and understandable.

③ Conferencing **

Teachers should meet with individual students to comment and give advice on assignments. Such meetings are called conferencing. Conferencing provides a student with a chance to discuss the strengths and weaknesses of his writing with the teacher. Teachers should remind students that academic progress rests on the student's shoulders and not the teacher's. When teachers are going over writing errors, they can prompt students for the corrections with hints or general error identification rather than provide the actual corrections themselves. During conferencing, the other students in the class can be assigned exercises or work on their assignments while the teacher meets with each individual.

④ Checklist **

The teacher can make a checklist which asks editors to check for the various areas in a piece of writing. It may ask editors, "Does the introduction contain a hook?", "Does the paper have a well-defined thesis?", "Do all the paragraphs have strong supporting sentences?", and so forth. It's best that teachers model an example of how to use this with an example well-written passage and a poorly written one and respond to them with a copy of this on an overhead projector for comparison.

⑤ Meaning-focused Feedback (Narrative Feedback) ***

Teachers can provide comments on content and organization to improve students' writing.

⑥ Form-focused Feedback: Error Correction Code (ECC) ***

This is a common tool to optimize learning opportunities from mistakes learners make in written work and to encourage the editing stages of process writing. Teachers show the learners where the mistakes are and what kind they are, and then learners try to correct the errors as a second stage to the initial writing task.

Chapter 06

06

03 Apply the Key Terms in Practice

1 Crucial Factors in Speaking

Read the teachers' conversation. Complete the table by filling in the descriptions and example classroom activities for each speaking component.

Mr. Choi : I've been thinking about how to improve my speaking lessons. Sometimes I'm not sure which aspects of speaking I should really focus on.

Ms. Park : That's a good question. Speaking is often described in terms of accuracy, fluency, and complexity.

Mr. Choi : Fluency sounds quite clear to me. It's about speaking smoothly without too many pauses, or hesitation, right? Activities like free discussion or storytelling would help students develop it.

Ms. Park : Exactly. On the other hand, accuracy is about using correct grammar, vocabulary, and pronunciation. For example, I sometimes use controlled speaking tasks, such as role-plays with set dialogues or short grammar-based drills, so students can practice correct forms.

Mr. Choi : Oh, I see. So accuracy requires tasks that guide students to produce more correct language.

Ms. Park : Right. And the third component, complexity, focuses on how varied and sophisticated their language is. Tasks like debates, problem-solving, or opinion-sharing push students to use more advanced structures and a wider range of vocabulary.

Mr. Choi : That makes sense. If I balance activities for accuracy, fluency, and complexity, my speaking lessons will become more effective.

Components	Descriptions	Example Classroom Activities
Accuracy	ⓐ _____ _____	ⓓ _____ _____
Fluency	ⓑ _____ _____	ⓔ _____ _____
Complexity	ⓒ _____ _____	ⓕ _____ _____

2 Communicative Tasks

Read the three students' learning logs about their classroom activities and follow the directions.

🔷 Student 1 – Jigsaw

"Today we worked on a reading task. Each group member read a different section of the article, and I focused on Part C. At first, I understood my own section well, but I couldn't complete the summary alone because I didn't know what was in the other parts. I had to listen carefully to my teammates and share my ideas too. Since we needed one complete summary, everyone's information was necessary. Without everyone's contribution, we couldn't finish the task, so I realized how important it was to work together."

🔷 Student 2 – Problem-solving

"Today we solved a puzzle to find out where the English club meeting will take place. Everyone got the same clues, so even if I didn't join the discussion, I could still figure out the answer by myself. I decided to talk with my partner anyway, and we confirmed that Room 103 was the only possible answer. Since the clues were clear, it wasn't necessary for everyone to participate, but sharing ideas made me feel more confident about the solution."

🔷 Student 3 – Decision-making

"In today's activity, we had to choose the best activity for next Friday's English club. We had three options, so I thought about my choice quietly first. Even if I didn't speak during the discussion, the group could still make a decision without me. In the end, I shared my opinion and we all agreed on the cooking workshop. It was okay not to participate, but I joined the talk because I wanted to explain my idea."

Based on the learning logs above, fill in the blanks with the most appropriate words.

🔲 Student 1

The jigsaw reading task involves ⓐ _____ interaction, because learners must exchange information to finish the summary. It is ⓑ _____ in goal-orientation, since the group works toward a single shared product. The outcome is ⓒ _____, as success depends on producing one complete and accurate summary of the article.

🔲 Student 2

The puzzle-solving activity shows ⓓ _____ interaction, since learners could reach the solution individually. It is ⓑ _____ in goal-orientation, as all students worked toward the same answer, and its outcome is ⓒ _____, because there was only one correct solution (Room 103).

🔲 Student 3

The activity shows ⓓ _____ interaction, because group members could reach a decision even without everyone's participation. It is ⓑ _____ in goal-orientation, as the group aimed for one shared choice, and its outcome is ⓔ _____ since the group could select any of the three options depending on discussion.

---

3 Teaching Pronunciation

Read the two teachers' teaching logs about their pronunciation lessons and fill in the blanks with the most appropriate terms.

⬦ Ms. Yoo's Teaching Log

Today, I applied a(n) ⓐ _____ approach in my pronunciation class. Instead of working on isolated sounds, I began with a short dialogue where meaning depended on ⓑ _____ features like stress, rhythm, and intonation. For example, students practiced the sentence *"I didn't say she stole the money"* and noticed how shifting the stress changed the meaning. I emphasized that ⓑ _____ often have a greater impact on ⓒ _____ than ⓔ _____, so mastering them can be more crucial for learners. Starting from meaningful context helped my students realize how pronunciation influences overall message delivery.

⬦ Mr. Kang's Teaching Log

In today's class, I used a(n) ⓓ _____ approach to teaching pronunciation. I focused on ⓔ _____ features, particularly the /r/ and /l/ distinction, which many of my students struggle with. To make practice meaningful, I provided ⓕ _____ such as *"I read a book"* vs. *"I led a group."* Students repeated them in short sentences and then used them in longer utterances. This step-by-step work on individual sounds helped build accuracy, but I noticed it sometimes took longer for students to connect these improvements to real-life communication.

---

4 Writing Approaches

Read the conversation between two teachers and fill in the blanks with the most appropriate terms.

Ms. Kim : Hey, Mr. Lee, I think my writing lessons aren't working well. I've been using a(n) ⓐ _____ approach, where students submit only one final draft. The problem is they don't get a chance to revise their writing, so their skills aren't improving. Many of them repeat the same mistakes, and some even lose confidence.

Mr. Lee : I understand. That's a common issue with ⓐ _____ writing. You might want to try ⓑ _____ writing instead. Students work through several stages–brainstorming, drafting, revising, and editing– which gives them more opportunities to improve step by step.

Ms. Kim : That sounds better than just grading the final product. But what about giving feedback? I don't want to overwhelm them.

Mr. Lee : That's where ⓒ _____ feedback comes in. Instead of marking every single error, you provide ⓓ _____ feedback by writing short comments explaining what they did well and what they can improve. For example, you might write, *'Your introduction is clear, but you could organize your supporting ideas more logically.'* This way, students focus on improving the content and flow.

Ms. Kim : I like that idea. But some of my students still need direct guidance on grammar and sentence structure.

Mr. Lee : Then you can combine it with ⓔ _____ feedback. Alongside narrative comments, you highlight specific language issues that affect meaning. One effective method is using a(n) ⓕ _____ instead of rewriting sentences for them. For example, you might underline an error and write "VT" for verb tense or "WW" for wrong word choice. Students then find and correct their own errors based on the code. It encourages active learning.

Ms. Kim : Oh, I see. So ⓓ _____ feedback helps students improve
ideas and organization, while the ⓕ _____ guides them to fix
language problems on their own.

Mr. Lee : Exactly. That way, students not only improve their writing but also
develop self-editing skills. It's more effective than simply giving a grade
on the final draft.

Ms. Kim : Thanks, Mr. Lee. I think I'll redesign my writing lessons using this
approach!

⑤ Writing Approach

Read the lesson plan and fill in the blank with the most appropriate words.

- Genre： Argumentative Essay
- Topic： "Should smartphones be allowed in school?"
- Subjects： 1st-grade high school students
- Objective： Students will learn to write an argumentative essay by understanding its purpose, structure, and language features, and then producing their own short essay.

◯ Teaching & Learning Cycle Steps for _____

Step 1. Group discussion or reading short articles with pros and cons about smartphones in school.

Step 2. Modeling the Genre
Analyze a rhetorical structure of an argumentative essay together.
① Highlight the Structure： Introduction with opinion / Reasons with supporting examples / Counterargument + Rebuttal / Conclusion
② Language Features (Connectors)： first, second, although, therefore

Step 3. Students write their own argumentative essay (100–150 words) on:

"Should smartphones be allowed in school?"

* Scaffold with an outline or sentence starters:

I think smartphones _ _ _ _ _ _ _ be allowed in school because...
First, ... / Second, ...
Some people say... but I think...
In conclusion, ...

---

6 Writing Activity (1)

Read the conversation below and fill in the blanks with the most appropriate words.

Ms. Kim : Okay, everyone. Today, we'll start with a short writing practice. Look at this worksheet. You see ten sentences in the present tense. Your job is to change the verbs into the past tense.

Students nod and look at their worksheets.

Minho : Teacher… like this? 'She goes to school' → 'She goed to school'?

Ms. Kim : Almost, Minho! Not 'goed,' but **'went.'** In this activity, there's only **one correct answer** for each blank, so you have to follow the grammar rules carefully.

Jisu : So… we don't write our own sentences?

Ms. Kim : Right. For now, we're practicing **accuracy**–how to use the correct verb forms. I'll give you the structure, and you just need to fill it in correctly. Don't worry about ideas yet.

Students work on changing the sentences using the correct verb forms.

Ms. Kim : Great job, everyone. This is called ⓐ _____. I control most of the sentences so you can focus on learning the correct forms.

Later in the same class, after finishing the task above.

Ms. Kim : Now, let's try something different. Look at these pictures of a boy's weekend trip. This time, you'll **write a short story** about what happened.

Jisu : Do we get the sentences like before?

Chapter 06

Ms. Kim : Not this time. I'll give you **some hints**, but you need to choose your own words. Here are some sentence starters:

'Last Saturday, I...'

'I went with...'

'We...'

Minho : So... we can make up our own details?

Ms. Kim : Exactly! You can write what the boy did, who he was with, and what happened next. You can **add your own ideas**, but the pictures and sentence starters will guide you.

Students begin writing their short stories using the sentence starters and pictures.

Ms. Kim : This is called ⓑ _____. I'm giving you a framework, but you're free to organize ideas and choose your own words. Focus on both **ideas** and **sentence structure**.

Jisu : This is harder... but also more fun!

Ms. Kim : Exactly. ⓐ _____ helps you practice grammar accurately, and ⓑ _____ helps you use those skills to create your own stories.

7 Writing Activity (2)

Read the two students' learning logs and identify the writing activity each student experienced, respectively.

🔖 Yujin's Learning Log

In today's writing lesson, the teacher read a short passage several times, and we were asked to rewrite it as accurately as possible without looking back at the text. At first, I was nervous because I thought I wouldn't remember everything, but focusing on the main ideas helped me recall more details than I expected. While writing, I realized the importance of **organizing the ideas logically** and **using correct grammar**, especially verb tenses and sentence structure. I also found that the **key words** provided on the board were really helpful for connecting the details and keeping the flow of the passage clear. Through this task, I learned how careful listening and structured writing can improve my accuracy.

🔖 Sooyoung's Learning Log

For homework, I was asked to keep **writing a journal** where I could share my thoughts, feelings, and daily experiences. After I submitted my entry, the teacher wrote back with short and encouraging comments responding to my ideas. I liked that the feedback focused more on the **content** rather than correcting every small grammar mistake, which made me feel less pressured and more confident when writing. It almost felt like having a **personal conversation** with the teacher through writing, and I realized I could express myself more openly without worrying too much about accuracy. This activity helped me see writing as a way to **communicate meaning** rather than something that only tests grammar.

Yujin – ⓐ _____

Sooyoung – ⓑ _____

Memo

Vocabulary &
Grammar

Map the Key Terms

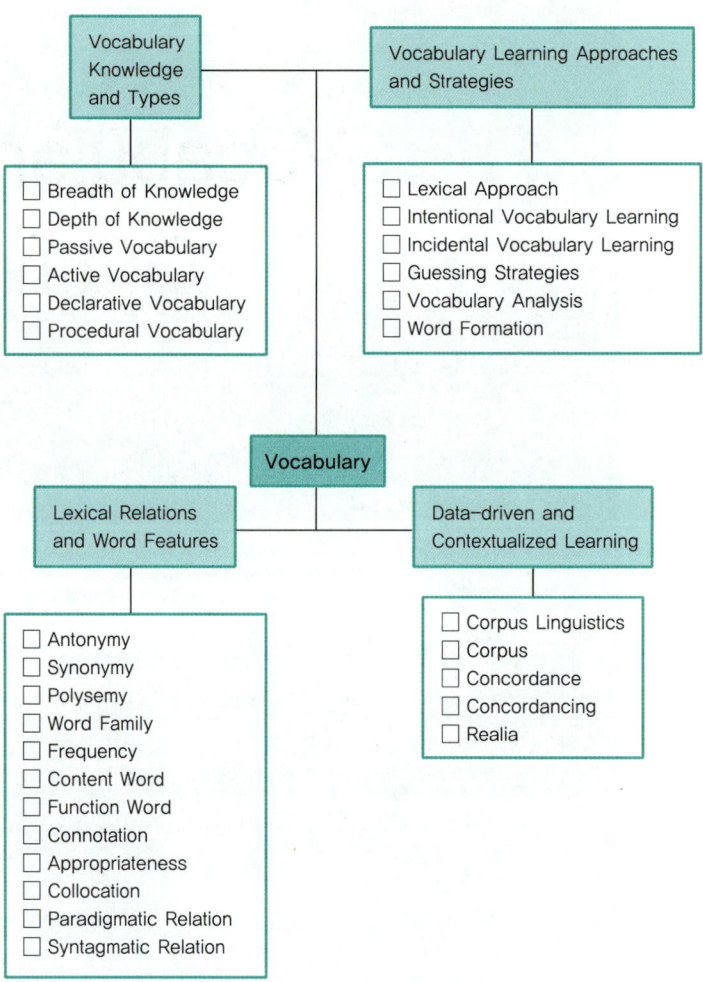

Vocabulary Knowledge and Types

- ☐ Breadth of Knowledge
- ☐ Depth of Knowledge
- ☐ Passive Vocabulary
- ☐ Active Vocabulary
- ☐ Declarative Vocabulary
- ☐ Procedural Vocabulary

Vocabulary Learning Approaches and Strategies

- ☐ Lexical Approach
- ☐ Intentional Vocabulary Learning
- ☐ Incidental Vocabulary Learning
- ☐ Guessing Strategies
- ☐ Vocabulary Analysis
- ☐ Word Formation

Vocabulary

Lexical Relations and Word Features

- ☐ Antonymy
- ☐ Synonymy
- ☐ Polysemy
- ☐ Word Family
- ☐ Frequency
- ☐ Content Word
- ☐ Function Word
- ☐ Connotation
- ☐ Appropriateness
- ☐ Collocation
- ☐ Paradigmatic Relation
- ☐ Syntagmatic Relation

Data-driven and Contextualized Learning

- ☐ Corpus Linguistics
- ☐ Corpus
- ☐ Concordance
- ☐ Concordancing
- ☐ Realia

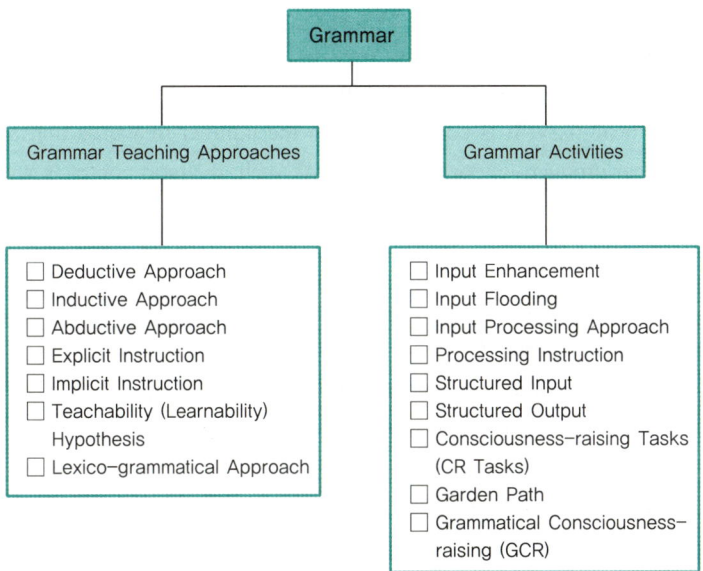

Master the Key Terms

❶ Vocabulary

(1) Vocabulary Knowledge and Types

① **Breadth of Knowledge** ★★★

This term is used primarily in vocabulary acquisition to refer to the size of a learner's vocabulary. It is concerned with the number of words that a learner knows, either productively or receptively. As such, the term contrasts with depth of knowledge, which refers to how much learners know about specific words. Some researchers argue that knowledge of the 3,000 most common words in a language will enable a learner to study in that language with relative ease.

② **Depth of Knowledge** 기출 ★★★

This is a term, primarily associated with vocabulary learning, that describes the amount of information that a learner knows about specific words. Learners may only know the basis form and meaning of a word, or they may have a deeper knowledge of the word, such as its derivational forms, its collocations or its connotations.

③ **Passive Vocabulary** ★★

The passive vocabulary consists of words we recognize and understand when reading a text or hearing them in speech.

④ **Active Vocabulary** ★★

The active vocabulary contains words that we can use in speaking and writing.

⑤ **Declarative Vocabulary** ★★★

Declarative vocabulary refers to explicit, conscious knowledge of words and their meanings, forms, and grammatical properties. It involves the ability to describe or define a word and to recall factual information about it.

⑥ **Procedural Vocabulary** ★★★

Procedural vocabulary refers to implicit, automatized knowledge that allows learners to use words fluently and accurately in real-time communication without conscious effort or explicit recall.

(2) Lexical Relations and Word Features

① Antonymy **

Antonymy refers to the relationship between words with opposite meanings. Examples include "hot" and "cold," or "fast" and "slow." Antonyms help learners understand word meanings through contrast.

② Synonymy **

Synonymy is the relationship between words that have similar or nearly the same meanings. For example, "big" and "large" are synonyms. However, perfect synonymy is rare since synonyms often carry different connotations or usage contexts.

③ Polysemy **

This refers to the phenomenon where a single word has multiple related meanings.

④ Word Family **

A word family includes a base word and all its derived and inflected forms, as well as related words formed by affixes. For example, the word family for "act" includes "action," "active," "actor," "react," and "inactive." Learning word families helps expand vocabulary efficiently by building on a known root.

⑤ Frequency ***

Frequency refers to how often a word appears in spoken or written language. High-frequency words are used very often and are typically learned early, while low-frequency words occur less commonly and may be more specialized. Word frequency affects how quickly and easily learners acquire and recall vocabulary.

⑥ Content Word *

words that carry the main meaning in a sentence, such as nouns, verbs, adjectives, and adverbs

⑦ Function Word *

words that have grammatical functions rather than carrying main meaning, such as prepositions, conjunctions, articles, and auxiliary verbs

Chapter 07

⑧ Connotation **

the additional meanings that a word or phrase has beyond its central meaning. These meanings show people's emotions and attitudes towards what the word or phrase refers to. Some connotations may be shared by a group of people of the same cultural or social background, sex, or age; others may be restricted to one or several individuals and depend on their personal experience.

⑨ Appropriateness ***

Using appropriate language means that a speaker's language is suitable or fitting for themselves, as the speaker; our audience; the speaking context; and the speech itself. Students need to know if a particular lexical item is usually used in writing or in speech; or in formal or informal discourse.

⑩ Collocation ***

A collocation is a group of words that often occur together. For example, in English one 'plays tennis' but 'goes skiing.' There are often no fixed rules for collocations and they are often one of the last components of vocabulary that L2 learners learn.

⑪ Paradigmatic Relation ***

Paradigmatic relation refers to the relationship between linguistic units (words or morphemes) that can substitute for each other in the same context or position within a sentence. In other words, they belong to the same category and can be replaced by one another without breaking the grammatical structure.

⑫ Syntagmatic Relation ***

Syntagmatic relation refers to the relationship between linguistic units that co-occur together in a sequence or linear order to form a syntactic structure. It describes how words combine with each other to form phrases or sentences.

(3) Vocabulary Learning Approaches and Strategies

① Lexical Approach **

a language teaching method that emphasizes the importance of words/vocabulary in SLA. The lexical approach is a way of analyzing and teaching language based on the idea that a language is made up of lexical units rather than grammatical structures. The units are words, chunks formed by collocations, and fixed phrases.

② Intentional Vocabulary Learning ★★★

This is the type of learning that learners consciously plan to do. It often involves the learning of specific grammar rules or vocabulary that are focused on in class. Intentional learning contrasts with incidental learning. Intentional learning is generally considered to be faster and more efficient than incidental learning, particularly when the topic to be learned is explicit information about the L2. However, there is less consensus about the benefits of intentional learning for the development of implicit L2 knowledge.

③ Incidental Vocabulary Learning 기출 ★★★

learning that happens without the learner intending for it to occur. For example, learners may be involved in a communicative activity in which they are discussing a specific topic. Thus, the primary intention is for them to practise speaking the L2. However, during that activity, a learner may notice and learn a specific lexical item or grammatical structure. Incidental exposure to lexical items is a by-product of communicative activities. Based on sufficient comprehensible input, learners' L2 vocabulary acquisition would largely take care of itself.

④ Guessing Strategies ★★★

Guessing strategies refer to learners' techniques for inferring the meaning of unknown words from context when reading or listening. These strategies are generally divided into two types: semantic context and grammatical context.

- Semantic Context: Learners use clues from the overall meaning of the sentence or paragraph, including surrounding words, topic, and prior knowledge.
  EX In the sentence "*The arid climate made farming difficult,*" a learner might guess "arid" means "dry" from the context of farming being difficult.
- Grammatical Context: Learners use clues from the grammatical structure, such as word forms, parts of speech, and syntactic roles, to infer meaning.
  EX In "*She is an accomplished pianist,*" knowing "accomplished" is an adjective that describes "pianist" helps a learner guess it means "skillful" or "experienced."

Chapter 07

⑤ Vocabulary Analysis ***

(a) Look for prefixes (co-, inter-, un-, etc.) that may give a clue.

(b) Look for suffixes (-tion, -tive, -ally, etc.) that may indicate what part of speech it is.

(c) Look for roots that are familiar. (ᴇx 'intervenire' may be a word that a student doesn't know, but recognizing that the root 'ven' comes from Latin 'to come' would yield the meaning 'to come in between'.)

⑥ Word Formation ***

Word formation is the process by which new words are formed by adding an affix, another word or converting from one word class to another by removing and adding letters. Derivation is the most common process of word formation. Derivation is accomplished when affixes (suffixes and prefixes) are added to words.

ᴇx 'dis- + respect + -ful = disrespectful', 'care + -less = careless'.

(4) Data-driven and Contextualized Learning

① Corpus Linguistics **

an approach to linguistic research that relies on computer analyses of a collection of text-written, transcribed speech or both stored in electronic form and analyzed with digital software

② Corpus ***

This is a collection of naturally occurring samples of language which have been collected and collated for easy access by researchers and materials developers who want to know how words and other linguistic items are actually used. A corpus may vary from a few sentences to a set of written texts or recordings.

③ Concordance **

It is an alphabetical list of the principal words used in a book or body of work, listing every stance of each word with its immediate context. The sample of concordance and provide students with instances of real language use helping learners to know how to use language that is appropriate in different contexts.

④ Concordancing ★★★

Concordancing is the indexing of words that enables one to reference words in the multiple possible contexts in which they appear in spoken or written language, thereby promoting consciousness-raising by drawing students' attention to formal elements of language within the context of meaningful communication and tasks. Concordancing allows learners to see words in context, while the extensive corpora serve as databanks that facilitate a deeper examination and understanding of the relationships between grammatical and lexical units.

⑤ Realia 기출 ★★★

Realia in EFL terms refers to any real objects we use in the classroom to bring the class to life.

② Grammar

(1) Grammar Teaching Approaches

① Deductive Approach 기출 ★★★

A deductive approach involves the learners being given a general rule, which is then applied to specific language examples and honed through practice exercises.

② Inductive Approach 기출 ★★★

An inductive approach involves the learners detecting, or noticing, patterns and working out a 'rule' for themselves before they practise the language.

③ Abductive Approach ★★★

Abduction refers to the exploratory process of trying out tentative solutions to problems or facts to figure out what may happen, to see if they work, or experience something new. In abductive learning, learners come to understand hidden rules of language use through the process of exploring hypotheses and inferences. This helps reinforce learning and encourages practical application of grammar in real-life situations.

④ Explicit Instruction ★★

language teaching that draws attention to language items and language rules in a clear manner and with the express purpose of teaching those linguistic items and rules. Explicit instruction involves the overt presentation of rules of the L2. This can be done both deductively and inductively.

⑤ Implicit Instruction ★★

language teaching in which learners are not overtly taught linguistic items. Learners' attention is not actively directed to specific language forms. In an implicit approach to grammar instruction, the teacher does not employ structural analysis or technical terms to explain the linguistic rules. Instead, the target form is used in the utterances made to communicate with the students.

⑥ Teachability (Learnability) Hypothesis *

Manfred Pienemann proposed that in order for linguistic structures to be learned, they must be relatively close to a learner's current interlanguage status. Structures that are too far beyond the learner's interlanguage are not teachable. Thus, he argued that the linguistic structures that are taught in the L2 classroom should follow the learner's stages of acquisition. However, there are some difficulties with such a proposal: (a) the stages of acquisition are known for only a limited number of linguistic structures in only a few languages; (b) learners within the same class may be at different stages of acquisition.

⑦ Lexico-grammatical Approach **

a view that lexis and grammar are two inherently connected parts of a single entity and should not be treated separately. "Vocabulary and grammatical structures are interdependent; so much so that it is possible to say with some justification that words have their own grammar." This interdependency of lexis and grammar is evident everywhere in language. For example, lexical verbs have valency (v+sth) patterns: some verbs can be used with a direct object, or with both a direct object and an indirect object, while others need no object at all.

(2) Grammar Activities

① Input Enhancement ***

Input enhancement is a focus on form task in which specific target structures are highlighted for the purpose of implicit instruction. Sharwood-Smith (1981) argues that internalization of the target forms, as well as meaning, occurs through improving the quality of input via typical input enhancement techniques such as *color-coding, boldfacing, underlining, italicizing, capitalizing*, and *highlighting* for textual enhancement purposes and oral repetition for aural enhancement purposes. It is claimed that this technique brings the forms into focal attention, and according to Schmidt (2001), some L2 components are so subtle and abstract that they cannot be attended to; therefore, one of the important functions of language teaching is to help focus learners' attention on the linguistic aspects.

Chapter 07

07

② Input Flooding ***

flooding learners with specific forms of the target language in order to draw learners' attention to the input. It presents texts that contain a target structure that appears frequently or repeatedly, and is therefore more salient. This may trigger syntactic priming, as speakers tend to "produce a previously spoken or heard structure."

③ Input Processing Approach ***

Input processing tries to provide an elaboration on how learners achieve 'form' from the input and how they parse sentences during the act of comprehension while their focal attention is on meaning. The overall aim of input processing tasks is to improve learners' intake which is not all input learners are exposed to, but the input learners actually comprehend in terms of form, function, and meaning. It is important that the text used for input remain reasonably natural, and that the learners make the necessary connections between form and function in authentic contexts of L2 use.

④ Processing Instruction **

a type of language teaching based on Bill VanPatten's input processing theory, which argues that learners use certain processing strategies to understand the L2. Processing instruction is entirely comprehension-based. Learners are given target language input but are not required to produce it.

⑤ Structured Input 기출 ***

a type of language that has been modified to draw learners' attention to specific linguistic forms. It is most frequently related to processing instruction, a method of language teaching that provides learners with language that has been manipulated to draw learners' attention to the fact that they may be relying on a strategy for processing language that does not work in the target language. Thus, it might contain language that cannot be understood correctly by using L1 strategies.

ex To determine subjects and objects in a sentence, learners must rely on word order in English, but the conjugations of the verbs in Spanish.

⑥ Structured Output 기출 ★★★

In terms of progression, structured output activities should follow structured input activities. Lee and VanPatten define structured output as "a special type of form-focused activity that is communicative in nature" (2003: 168). They provide two major characteristics of structured output activities:

(a) They involve the exchange of previously unknown information.

(b) They require learners to access a particular form or structure in order to express meaning.

⑦ Consciousness-raising Tasks (CR Tasks) ★★★

Ellis et al. (2001) define consciousness-raising tasks as a pedagogic activity where the learners are provided with second language data in some form and required to perform some operation on it, the purpose of which is to arrive at an explicit understanding of the target grammar. The consciousness-raising tasks seem to be similar to the PPP (presentation, practice, production) model, but one significant difference is clear. In the PPP model, students are required to use a target form in speaking or writing. However, in consciousness-raising tasks what learners should be able to do is not to use the form in speaking and writing, but to find the rule and understand the target form in terms of form, meaning, and function.

⑧ Garden Path ★★★

In the garden path, which is the most explicit technique, a teacher takes learners into making overgeneralization regarding a grammatical rule so that the learners can notice the form more impressively. That is, when a teacher plans to teach a certain target form, the teacher only briefly explains the major rules of the form instead of its exceptions. Then, the teacher corrects students' errors, providing the rule of the exceptions when students' overgeneralization actually occur.

⑨ Grammatical Consciousness-raising (GCR) ★★★

a language teaching approach where learners are exposed to language data, challenged to analyze it, and develop their own understanding of grammatical rules, rather than being directly taught the rules.

03 Apply the Key Terms in Practice

1 Teaching Vocabulary

Read the conversation between the teacher and the student and fill in the blanks with the most appropriate terms.

Jisu : Teacher, I study so many new words, but I still forget them quickly. How can I improve my vocabulary?

Ms. Kim : That's a common problem. First, think about vocabulary ⓐ _____ and vocabulary ⓑ _____. Do you know the difference?

Jisu : Not really. What's the difference?

Ms. Kim : ⓐ _____ is about how many words you know–the size of your vocabulary. ⓑ _____ is about how well you know each word. For example, you might know the meaning of the word '**bank**', but do you also know all its other meanings and how to use it naturally?

Jisu : Oh, so knowing many words isn't enough. I also need to know them deeply.

Ms. Kim : Exactly. ⓑ _____ includes understanding a word's ⓒ _____, ⓓ _____, and even how frequently it's used.

Jisu : ⓒ _____? What's that?

Ms. Kim : They are words that naturally go together. For example, we say '**make a decision**', not '**do a decision**'. If you know the right collocations, your sentences will sound more natural.

Jisu : Ah, I see. And you mentioned ⓓ _____ too, right?

Ms. Kim : Yes. ⓓ _____ is when one word has multiple meanings. For example, '**bank**' can mean a place where you keep money, or the side of a river. Knowing these different meanings helps you understand words in different contexts.

Jisu : That makes sense. But sometimes I don't know which meaning is more common.

Ms. Kim : Good point. That's where ⓔ _____ comes in. Some meanings–and even some words–are used much more often than others. For example, the meaning of '**bank**' as a '**money place**' is far more frequent than 'river bank.' If you focus on **high-frequency words** and their most common meanings first, you can understand more texts and conversations and improve your vocabulary faster.

Jisu : So studying ⓔ _____ helps me choose which words and meanings to focus on first?

Ms. Kim : Exactly! ⓔ _____ gives you a sense of **priority**, so you learn the words you'll actually need and use most.

Jisu : That's helpful. But what about those long words lists I study? I still mix up words sometimes.

Ms. Kim : That's normal. To improve, don't just memorize meanings. Try to learn common ⓒ _____, practice using the words in your own sentences, and focus on high-ⓔ _____ words you'll actually use.

❷ Collocations

Read the conversation between the teacher and the students and fill in the blanks with the most appropriate terms.

Ms. Yoo ： Today, we're learning about ⓐ _____. Look at this example： we say '**make a decision**'. Does anyone know why we don't usually say '**do a decision**'?

Seojin ： I thought they mean the same. 'Do a decision' sounds okay to me.

Ms. Yoo ： That's a good guess, but ⓐ _____ are about **which words sound natural together**. Even though 'make' and 'do' are both verbs, only 'make a decision' sounds natural. To understand why, we need to look at two relations： ⓑ _____ and ⓒ _____.

Jihun ： Oh... two relations?

Ms. Yoo ： First, the ⓑ _____ relation is about **words that naturally combine**. For example, 'make + decision' is a strong pair because these two words frequently appear together in English.

Seojin ： So ⓑ _____ means we look at words that usually go together?

Ms. Yoo ： Exactly! Now, the ⓒ _____ relation is different. It's about **what other words you could choose in the same position**. For example, instead of 'make a decision', you could also say 'reach a decision' or, in British English, 'take a decision'. But 'do a decision' sounds unnatural because native speakers rarely use it.

Jihun ： Oh, so ⓑ _____ shows **which words combine**, and ⓒ _____ shows **what words we can choose from**?

Teacher ： Exactly! That's why we prefer '**make a decision**'–it's the most natural choice among possible options.

3 Intentional vs. Incidental Learning

Read the conversation between two teachers and fill in each blank with the most appropriate term.

Ms. Kim : I've been focusing on vocabulary this week, but I'm not sure if my method works. I taught word families yesterday as part of ⓐ _____ vocabulary learning.

Mr. Lee : Oh, like showing students how *'act'* connects to *'action'*, *'active'*, and *'activity'*?

Ms. Kim : Exactly! I gave them a chart, explained the meanings, and had them make sentences using at least three forms. But I'm worried they might forget them after a few days.

Mr. Lee : Yeah, that happens a lot with ⓐ _____ learning. That's why I also encourage extensive reading for ⓑ _____ vocabulary learning.

Ms. Kim : Do your students actually pick up new words just by reading?

Mr. Lee : Surprisingly, yes. They choose books or online articles they're interested in, so they're more motivated. One student read a K-pop article and kept seeing the word *'performance'* and later noticed its related forms like *'perform'* and *'performer'* in other contexts–without me directly teaching them.

Ms. Kim : Ah, I see. So in extensive reading, students naturally meet words repeatedly in different contexts, and that reinforces learning without direct instruction.

Mr. Lee : Exactly.

4 Techniques for Vocabulary

Read the comments from four students and then identify the most suitable vocabulary learning technique for each student, respectively.

🔶 **Jisoo**

Whenever I study new words, I usually memorize their meanings but didn't know how to actually use it. I think it would help if I focused on one word at a time and looked at its definition, synonyms, antonyms, common collocations, and example sentences. For instance, I could learn that '**house**' means 'a building where people live,' its synonyms are '**home**' and '**residence**', its antonyms are '**store**' and '**office**', and useful collocations include '**rent a house**' and '**big house.**' Then, I could practice sentences like "*My friend bought a new house near the park.*" I believe this would help me understand the word more deeply and remember it better.

🔶 **Minho**

When I learn a new word, I often don't know which other words usually go with it. For example, I know the word '**heavy**', but I didn't know I should say '**heavy rain**' and '**heavy traffic**', not '**big rain**' or '**big traffic**'. I want to learn groups of words that naturally go together, so I can remember and use them more easily. If I study these related expressions together, I think my speaking will sound more natural.

🔶 **Hana**

I often get confused when different forms of the same word appear in texts. For example, I know the verb '**educate**', but I have trouble understanding '**education**', '**educational**', and '**educator**'. I wish I could learn all these forms together instead of studying them separately. That way, I can use the right form in my writing and speaking.

⬡ Taeyang

I sometimes feel frustrated because I know some adjectives but don't know how to turn them into verbs. For example, I know the word '**wide**', but I didn't realize I could make the verb '**widen**' by adding '**-en**'. I want to learn more rules like this so I can create different word forms by myself. I think it would help me express my ideas more flexibly when writing and speaking.

Jisoo – ⓐ _____

Minho – ⓑ _____

Hana – ⓒ _____

Taeyang – ⓓ _____

❺ Teaching Collocation Using Concordancer

Read the lesson procedure and fill in the blanks with the most appropriate terms.

📦 Lesson Procedure

Step 1. Setting the Context
T explains that Ss often use unnatural expressions in their writing, such as *"do a decision"* instead of *"make a decision"*, and introduces ⓐ _____ as essential for producing more natural language.

Step 2. Introducing the Task
Ss are told that they will engage in ⓑ _____ vocabulary learning by exploring authentic language data to discover correct ⓐ _____ for target words.

Step 3. Using a(n) ⓒ _____
T provides access to an online ⓒ _____ and explains that it contains real examples of language use collected from various authentic texts.

Step 4. Searching with a(n) ⓓ _____
Ss use a(n) ⓓ _____ to search for the target words (e.g., *decision, rain, progress*) and analyze concordance lines to identify the most frequent and natural ⓐ _____.

Step 5. Noticing and Recording Patterns
In pairs, Ss discuss their findings and make a list of correct ⓐ _____, reinforcing their learning through active comparison of authentic examples.

Step 6. Application Activity
Ss complete a short writing task where they use the newly learned ⓐ _____, applying their ⓑ _____ vocabulary learning to produce more accurate and fluent sentences.

---

6 Grammar Teaching Approaches (1)

Read the teachers' teaching log and identify grammar teaching approaches that each teacher applied, respectively.

⬡ Teacher 1

Today, I explicitly **introduced the rule** for the past perfect tense first. I wrote on the board:

"Subject + had + past participle."

Then I explained that we use the past perfect to describe an action that happened **before another past action**. After the explanation, I gave students example sentences like:

"I had finished my homework before my mom came home."
"She had already left when I arrived."

Finally, students practiced by completing a short worksheet. I noticed they could apply the form quickly because the rule was **clear from the start**, but a few still struggled to use it in spontaneous speaking.

⬡ Teacher 2

In my class, I first gave my students a handout with a short dialogue that included the present perfect and the past simple, and then asked them to discover the implied rule themselves.

Dialogue A

A : *Have you ever tried Mexican food?*
B : *Yes, I have. It was delicious.*

Dialogue B

A : *Did you go to Mexico last summer?*
B : *Yes, I went with my family.*

In groups, students analyzed the dialogues and tried to figure out the difference between *"Have you ever tried"* and *"Did you go"*. After discussion, each group presented their findings.

I then provided new examples for students to test their rules. After they tested their hypotheses, I helped them refine and confirm the rule:

Present Perfect → experience without specific time
Past Simple → completed action with a specific time

Students seemed more engaged because they **found the rule themselves**, but it took extra time for them to arrive at the right conclusion.

Teacher 1 – ⓐ _____ Approach
Teacher 2 – ⓑ _____ Approach

7 Grammar Teaching Approaches (2)

Read the grammar lesson plan and fill in the blanks with the most appropriate term.

◻ _____ Grammar Lesson Plan (Present Perfect)

Target Form: have/has + past participle

Level: Middle school (intermediate)

Time: 40 minutes

1. Introduction – Authentic Input (5 minutes)

- T shows students a short authentic dialogue (e.g., from a blog or transcript):

  A : Have you ever been to Japan?

  B : Yes, I've been there twice. I went last year and two years ago.

  A : Really? I haven't been there yet.

- T reads it aloud naturally and asks:

  "What are they talking about?" (general meaning check)

  "Which words show they are talking about past experiences?"

2. Guided Output – Personalization (10 minutes)

- Ss pair up and ask each other similar questions about routines or experiences:

  "Have you ever tried sushi?"

  "Have you ever been to Jeju?"

  "What did you do last weekend?"

- T circulates, listening but not explaining rules yet.

3. Group Discussion – Hypothesis Building (10 minutes)

• In small groups, Ss compare the sentences they used.

• T prompts:

"Why do we say 'I have been to Jeju' but 'I went to Jeju last year'?"

"What's the difference?"

• Groups brainstorm and suggest hypotheses, e.g.:

"Present perfect = experience, no specific time."

"Past simple = action with a clear past time."

→ *This is the _____ reasoning step∶ learners make the best explanation for the difference based on incomplete but meaningful evidence.*

4. Teacher Clarification – Confirmation (10 minutes)

• T collects student ideas on the board and confirms the main rule:

- **Present Perfect** = have/has + past participle, used for experiences without a specific time, or situations connected to now.
- **Past Simple** = verb + -ed/irregular form, used for actions at a definite past time.

• T highlights student contributions that matched the correct explanation.

5. Wrap-up and Practice (5 minutes)

• Quick "Find Someone Who…" game:

"Find someone who has eaten sushi."

"Find someone who went abroad last year."

• Ss walk around, ask/answer, and apply both forms.

8 Grammar Activities (1)

Read the conversation between two teachers and fill in the blanks with the most appropriate terms.

Ms. Park : Mr. Choi, I've noticed that many of my students still struggle with the present perfect. Even after my lesson, they keep switching to the simple past.

Mr. Choi : I've seen the same in my class. I think the issue is that students often don't really ⓐ _____ the target form when they're reading or listening.

Ms. Park : Exactly. They focus on meaning and ignore the structure completely. We need to make the form stand out more somehow.

Mr. Choi : One way to do that is ⓑ _____. For example, we can bold or underline the present perfect forms in the text so they become more ⓒ _____. That visual emphasis can naturally guide students' attention to the pattern.

Ms. Park : That makes sense. So, instead of explaining the rule directly, we let the text itself highlight it.

Mr. Choi : Right. But we also need to give them plenty of examples. If the text includes many sentences with the present perfect, students will get repeated exposure. That's called ⓓ _____, and it helps learners process the pattern more implicitly.

Ms. Park : Ah, so enhancement helps students ⓐ _____ the form, and flooding provides enough repetition for them to internalize it.

Mr. Choi : Exactly. When we combine both strategies, students can start recognizing patterns without feeling overwhelmed by explicit grammar rules.

Ms. Park : I like that. For my next class, I'll prepare a short article filled with present perfect examples and highlight the key forms to make them more noticeable.

Mr. Choi : Great idea. I'll try the same approach and we can compare how our students respond next week.

---

⑨ Grammar Activities (2)

Read the instruction below and fill in the blanks with the most appropriate terms.

- Grammar Instruction Based on ⓐ _____
- Target Form : Past Tense – Regular Verbs (e.g., walked, played, watched)
- Subjects : Korean 2nd-grade middle school students
- Communicative Goal : Understanding and identifying actions that happened in the past based on context and time cues.

◻ ⓑ _____ Sequence

Step 1. Explicit Information (Grammar Explanation in Input Terms)

"In English, we add -ed to a verb to show that something happened in the past. For example, play → played. But English learners sometimes don't notice this -ed because they focus more on the subject or the object."

Step 2. ⓒ _____ Activity

→ Students listen to Minhee's weekly log and figure out what she did last week.
→ Students read two similar sentences and choose the one that matches the meaning of a visual context.

Visual Context : "Minhee played the piano last weekend."

Which sentence matches this?

a) "Minhee plays the piano."
b) "Minhee played the piano."

⑩ Grammar Activities (3)

Read the task below, and identify what type of the task it is.

📦 Task Sheet for Student A

Student A

1. Look at the table below. The adjectives are in italics, and the comparative/ superlative forms are in bold.

2. You need to work with your partner to complete the table. Ask your partner to read out his/her sentences. Listen carefully, then write them down in the appropriate column in your table.

3. Talk about the sentences. Why are the sentences in the second column incorrect? Complete the rules in the final column by filling in the blanks.

No	Correct	Incorrect	Explanation of Incorrect Sentences
1	• This book is **more** *interesting* than that one. • The movie was **more** *exciting* than I expected.		Don't add _ _ _ _ _ to adjectives with _ _ _ _ _ syllables. Use _ _ _ _ _ + adjective instead.
2		• Tom is the **most** *tall* student in the class. • This is the **most** *happiest* day of my life.	Don't use _ _ _ _ _ with adjectives that already take _ _ _ _ _. Use either _ _ _ _ or _ _ _ _, not both.
3	• This question is *easier* than the last one. • My bag is *heavier* than yours.		Don't use _ _ _ _ together with the _ _ _ _ _ form. Choose only one.

4. Now write down a sentence of your own for each of these rules.

⓫ Grammar Activities (4)

Read the conversation between two teachers and fill in the blanks with the most appropriate terms.

Mr. Kim　：Do you have a minute, Ms. Park? I'd like to hear your thoughts on teaching grammar more effectively.

Ms. Park　：Of course! What's the challenge?

Mr. Kim　：My students memorize rules, but they struggle whenever there are exceptions. Do you have any strategies that work well?

Ms. Park　：Actually, yes. I've recently been using ⓐ _____ strategy in my grammar lessons.

Mr. Kim　：Is that the one **where students make errors by overgeneralizing grammar rules** and adjust their understanding using the **partial information** you provide?

Ms. Park　：Exactly! This way, they can **discover the exceptions**, which makes the rules easier to remember.

Mr. Kim　：Ah, I see. So, it's a(n) ⓑ _____ approach **where students figure out a general rule from several examples**, right?

Ms. Park　：That's right. Students observe the examples and find the rule on their own, which helps them remember it better.

Mr. Kim　：Sounds great! I think I'll try this method in my next lesson.

Answers

1 Teaching Vocabulary

ⓐ breadth / Breadth
ⓑ depth / Depth
ⓒ collocations / Collocations
ⓓ polysemy / Polysemy
ⓔ frequency / Frequency

2 Collocations

ⓐ collocations
ⓑ syntagmatic
ⓒ paradigmatic

3 Intentional vs. Incidental Learning

ⓐ intentional
ⓑ incidental

4 Techniques for Vocabulary

ⓐ Word Map
ⓑ Word Association
ⓒ Word Family
ⓓ Word Formation

5 Teaching Collocation Using Concordancer

ⓐ collocations
ⓑ intentional
ⓒ Corpus / corpus
ⓓ Concordancer / concordancer

6 Grammar Teaching Approaches (1)

ⓐ Deductive
ⓑ Inductive

7 Grammar Teaching Approaches (2)

Abductive / abductive

8 Grammar Activities (1)

ⓐ notice
ⓑ input enhancement
ⓒ salient
ⓓ input flooding

9 Grammar Activities (2)

ⓐ Input Processing
ⓑ Processing Instruction
ⓒ Structured Input

10 Grammar Activities (3)

Consciousness-raising Task

11 Grammar Activities (4)

ⓐ garden path
ⓑ inductive

Chapter 07

Assessment

Principles

- ☐ Practicality
- ☐ Reliability
- ☐ Student−related Reliability
- ☐ Administration Reliability
- ☐ Inter−rater Reliability
- ☐ Intra−rater Reliability
- ☐ Internal Consistency
- ☐ Split−half Reliability
- ☐ Validity
- ☐ Content Validity
- ☐ Face Validity
- ☐ Construct Validity
- ☐ Criterion−related Validity
- ☐ Concurrent Validity
- ☐ Predictive Validity
- ☐ Authenticity
- ☐ Washback

Types of Assessment

- ☐ Formative Test
- ☐ Summative Test
- ☐ Direct Test
- ☐ Indirect Test
- ☐ Objective Test
- ☐ Subjective Test
- ☐ Norm−referenced Assessment
- ☐ Criterion−referenced Assessment
- ☐ Discrete−point Testing
- ☐ Integrative Testing
- ☐ Cloze Test
- ☐ Fixed−ratio Deletion
- ☐ Rational Deletion
- ☐ Gap−filling Procedure
- ☐ Exact Word Method
- ☐ Acceptable Word Method (Appropriate Word Scoring)
- ☐ C−test

Purpose of Assessment

- ☐ Proficiency Test
- ☐ Diagnostic Test
- ☐ Placement Test
- ☐ Achievement Test
- ☐ Progress Test
- ☐ Screen Test

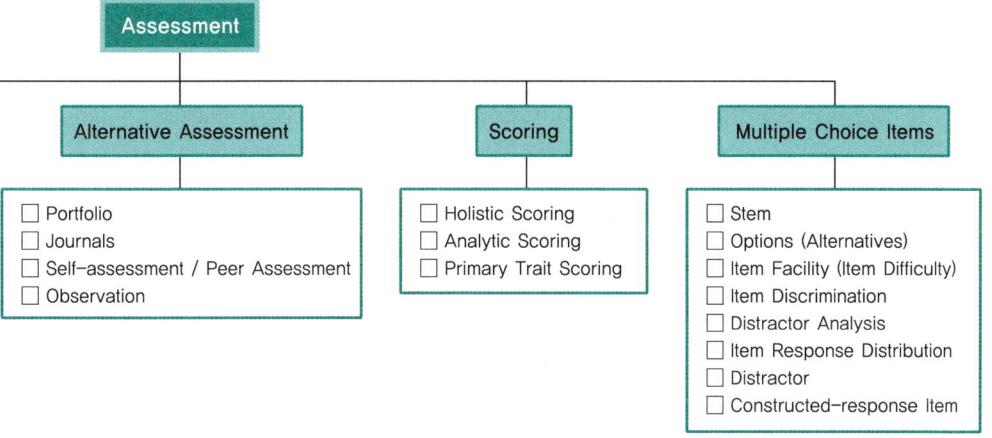

Assessment

Alternative Assessment
- ☐ Portfolio
- ☐ Journals
- ☐ Self-assessment / Peer Assessment
- ☐ Observation

Scoring
- ☐ Holistic Scoring
- ☐ Analytic Scoring
- ☐ Primary Trait Scoring

Multiple Choice Items
- ☐ Stem
- ☐ Options (Alternatives)
- ☐ Item Facility (Item Difficulty)
- ☐ Item Discrimination
- ☐ Distractor Analysis
- ☐ Item Response Distribution
- ☐ Distractor
- ☐ Constructed-response Item

Master the Key Terms

(1) Principles

① Practicality 기출 ★★★

the extent to which an instrument is within desirable financial limitations, time constraints, and ease of administration, scoring, and interpretation

② Reliability 기출 ★★★

A test is consistent and dependable. If you give the same test to the same student or matched students on two different occasions, the test should yield similar results.

③ Student-related Reliability ★★

The most common learner-related issue in reliability is caused by temporary illness, fatigue, a "bad day," anxiety, and other physical or psychological factors, which may make an "observed" score deviate from one's "true" score.

④ Administration Reliability ★★

Administration reliability refers to the extent to which test results are consistent and not influenced by external factors related to the conditions of test administration. Poor administration reliability occurs when environmental or procedural factors—such as noise, lighting, temperature, or equipment—interfere with test-takers' ability to perform accurately, leading to unreliable or invalid results.

⑤ Inter-rater Reliability 기출 ★★★

Human error, subjectivity, and bias may enter into the scoring process. Low inter-rater reliability occurs when two or more scorers yield inconsistent scores of the same test, possibly for lack of attention to scoring criteria, inexperience, inattention, or even preconceived biases.

⑥ Intra-rater Reliability 기출 ★★★

the degree of agreement among repeated administrations of a diagnostic test performed by a single rater

⑦ Internal Consistency ★★★

Internal consistency reliability looks at each item in a test that measures the same content. It assesses the correlation between multiple items in a test that are intended to measure the same construct. Internal consistency reliability is a type of reliability used to determine the validity of similar items on a test. All questions on a test proposed to measure certain content should produce similar and consistent results. Researchers use internal consistency reliability to ensure that each item on a test is related to the topic they are researching. Ensuring items on a test are relevant to the study and measure the same construct ensures that the test is valid. As a result, other researchers can depend on the results. Not having consistent reliability in a study renders the test results invalid.

⑧ Split-half Reliability ★★★

This refers to a measure of internal consistency obtained by correlating two halves of a test (ex odd vs. even items) to assess how consistently the test measures a construct.

⑨ Validity ★★★

the extent to which inferences made from assessment results are appropriate, meaningful, and useful in terms of the purpose of the assessment

⑩ Content Validity ★★★

If a test actually samples the subject matter about which conclusions are to be drawn, and if it requires the test-taker to perform the behavior that is being measured, it can claim content-related evidence of validity, often popularly referred to as content validity.

⑪ Face Validity **

the extent to which students view the assessment as fair, relevant, and useful for improving learning. Face validity means that students perceive the test to be valid. It will be perceived valid if it samples the actual content of what learners have achieved or expect to achieve.

⑫ Construct Validity ***

A construct is any theory, hypothesis, or model that attempts to explain observed phenomena in our universe of perceptions. "Proficiency" and "communicative competence" are linguistic constructs. Construct validity asks, "Does this test actually tap into the theoretical construct as it has been defined?"

⑬ Criterion-related Validity 기출 **

the extent to which the "criterion" of the test has actually been reached. In the case of teacher-made classroom assessments, criterion-related evidence is best demonstrated through a comparison of results of an assessment with results of some other measure of the same criterion.

⑭ Concurrent Validity ***

A test has concurrent validity if its results are supported by other concurrent performance.

⑮ Predictive Validity ***

The predictive validity of an assessment becomes important in the case of placement tests, admissions assessment batteries, language aptitude tests, and the like. The assessment criterion in such cases is not to measure concurrent ability but to assess (and predict) a test-taker's likelihood of future success.

⑯ Authenticity 기출 ***

the degree of correspondence of the characteristics of a given language test task to the features of a target language task. Essentially, when you make a claim for authenticity in a test task, you are saying that this task is likely to be enacted in the "real world."

⑰ Washback 기출 ★★★

the effects, both beneficial and detrimental, of an assessment on teaching and learning prior to and after the assessment itself. When students take a test, ideally they will receive feedback about their competence, based on their performance. The feedback should "wash back" to them in the form of useful diagnoses of strengths and weaknesses. In the case of informal assessment, it is more likely to have built-in washback effects by nature, because the teacher usually provides interactive feedback. A formal test also can have positive washback, but it is also subject to an absence of washback if students simply receive a letter grade or a single overall numerical score.

(2) Types of Assessment

① Formative Test ★★★

Formative assessment is used to aid learning. In an educational setting, formative assessment might be a teacher (or peer) or the learner providing feedback on a student's work, and would not necessarily be used for grading purposes. Formative assessments are diagnostic.

② Summative Test ★★

Summative assessment is generally carried out at the end of a course or project. In an educational setting, summative assessments are typically used to assign students a course grade. These types of assessments are generally evaluative.

③ Direct Test ★

Direct testing involves the test-taker in actually performing the target task.

④ Indirect Test ★

In an indirect test, learners are not performing the task itself but rather a task that is related in some way.

⑤ Objective Test *

Objective assessment is a form of questioning that has a single correct answer.

EX multiple choice, true or false answers, matching questions

⑥ Subjective Test *

Subjective assessment is a form of questioning that may have more than one correct answer (or more than one way of expressing the correct answer).

EX extended-response questions, essays

⑦ Norm-referenced Assessment ★★★

Norm-referenced assessment (colloquially known as "grading on the curve") is not measured against defined criteria. This type of assessment is relative to the student body undertaking the assessment.

⑧ Criterion-referenced Assessment ★★★

This occurs when candidates are measured against defined (and objective) criteria. It is designed to give test-takers feedback on specific course or lesson objectives. The best known example of a criterion-referenced assessment is the driving test.

⑨ Discrete-point Testing ★★★

Language is segmented into many small linguistic points and the four language skills of listening, speaking, reading, and writing. Test questions are designed to test these skills and linguistic points. A discrete point test consists of many questions on a large number of linguistic points, but each question tests only one linguistic point. Such tests have a downside in that they take language out of context and usually bear no relationship to the concept or use of the whole language.

EX multiple choice, grammar item

⑩ Integrative Testing 기출 ★★★

Integrative tests attempt to assess a learner's capacity to use many bits all at the same time, and possibly while exercising several presumed components of a grammatical system, and perhaps more than one of the traditional skills or aspects of skills.

EX interviews, cloze test

⑪ Cloze Test 기출 ★★★

In written language, a sentence with a word left out should have enough context that a reader can close that gap with a calculated guess, using linguistic expectancies (formal schemata), background experience (content schemata), and some strategic competence.

⑫ Fixed-ratio Deletion ★★★

Typically every seventh word (plus or minus two) is deleted.

⑬ Rational Deletion ★★★

Choose deletions according to the grammatical or discourse functions of the words.

⑭ Gap-filling Procedure ★★

an assessment task where learners fill in missing words or phrases in a sentence or passage. It evaluates their ability to use grammatical knowledge, vocabulary, and contextual clues to produce meaningful language.

⑮ Exact Word Method ★★

Students get credit for a correct answer if and only if the word they write in any given blank is the exact word deleted from the original text. This approach is quick and, therefore, very practical, and also highly reliable.

⑯ Acceptable Word Method (Appropriate Word Scoring) ★★

Any response that is grammatically correct and makes good sense in the context is given full credit as an acceptable answer. This method may promote positive washback, since it could encourage learners to use their pragmatic expectancy grammars creatively.

⑰ C-test ★★★

The second half (according to the number of letters) of every other word is obliterated, and the test-taker must restore each word.

(3) Purpose of Assessment

① Proficiency Test **

If your aim in a test is to tap global competence in a language, then you are testing proficiency. Proficiency tests have traditionally consisted of standardized multiple-choice items on grammar, vocabulary, reading comprehension, aural comprehension, and sometimes on a sample of writing. Such tests often have content validity weaknesses, but after several decades of construct validation research, some great strides have been made toward constructing communicative proficiency tests.

② Diagnostic Test 기출 ***

This test is designed to diagnose a particular aspect of a language. A diagnostic test has the purpose of determining which features of English are difficult for a learner and should therefore become a part of a curriculum. These tests offer a checklist of features for the administrator to use in pinpointing difficulties. It is not advisable to use a general achievement test as a diagnostic, since diagnostic tests need to be specifically tailored to offer information on student need that will be worked on imminently. Achievement tests are useful in analyzing the extent to which students have acquired language features that have already been taught.

③ Placement Test **

Certain proficiency tests and diagnostic tests can act in the role of placement tests, whose purpose is to place a student into an appropriate level or section of a language curriculum or school. A placement test typically includes a sampling of material to be covered in the curriculum (that is, it has content validity), and it thereby provides an indication of the point at which the student will find a level of class to be neither too easy nor too difficult, but appropriately challenging.

④ Achievement Test **

An achievement test is related directly to classroom lessons, units, or even a total curriculum. Achievement tests are limited to particular material covered in a curriculum within a particular time frame, and are offered after a course has covered the objectives in question. Achievement tests can serve as indicators of features that a student needs to work on in the future, but the primary role of an achievement test is to determine acquisition of course objectives at the end of a period of instruction.

⑤ Progress Test **

A progress test is an assessment given during a course to measure how well learners have understood and retained material covered so far, providing feedback for both students and teachers.

⑥ Screen Test *

A screen test is a preliminary assessment used to quickly identify whether learners meet certain criteria or possess a basic level of ability before further evaluation or placement.

(4) Alternative Assessment

① Portfolio 기출 ***

A portfolio is a purposeful collection of students' work that demonstrates their efforts, progress, and achievements in given areas.

② Journals ***

A journal is a log (or "account") of one's thoughts, feelings, reactions, assessments, ideas, or progress toward goals, usually written with little attention to structure, form, or correctness. Learners can articulate their thoughts without the threat of those thoughts being judged later (usually by the teacher).

③ Self-assessment / Peer Assessment ***

Students are usually frank and honest in their assessment of their own performance and that of their peers. Peer assessment supports students and teachers alike, reduces workload and increases engagement and understanding. Student insights and observations are valued. They are important because they help the students reflect on and understand the process of their own learning.

④ Observation **

a valuable assessment method that involves systematically watching and recording a learner's performance, behavior, and interactions in a natural setting to gain insights into their abilities and progress

(5) Scoring

① Holistic Scoring ***

It uses a rubric for scoring oral production holistically. Each point on a holistic scale is given a systematic set of descriptors, and the reader-evaluator matches an overall impression with the descriptors to arrive at a score.

② Analytic Scoring ***

For classroom instruction, holistic scoring provides little washback into the writer's further stages of learning. Classroom evaluation of learning is best served through analytic scoring, in which multiple major elements of writing are scored, thus enabling learners to capture their weaknesses and strengths.

③ Primary Trait Scoring **

Primary trait scoring refers to an assessment approach in which a single, most important criterion (or trait) relevant to the specific task is selected and used as the primary basis for scoring. This method focuses on how well the student achieves the main communicative purpose of the task.

(6) Multiple Choice Items

① Stem *

the part of a multiple choice item that presents the question or problem that test-takers need to answer

② Options (Alternatives) *

the set of possible answers presented in a multiple-choice item, including one correct answer and several distractors

③ Item Facility (Item Difficulty) ***

Item facility (IF) is the extent to which an item is easy or difficult for the proposed group of test-takers.

④ Item Discrimination 기출 ★★★

This is the extent to which an item differentiates between high- and low-ability test-takers. If a test is given to a large group of people, the discriminating power of an item can be measured by comparing the number of people with high test scores who answered that item correctly with the number of people with low scores who answered the same item correctly. If a particular item is doing a good job of discriminating between those who score high and those who score low, more people in the top-scoring group will have answered the item correctly.

⑤ Distractor Analysis ★★★

Analyzing the distractors (ex incorrect alternatives) is useful in determining the relative usefulness of the decoys in each item.

⑥ Item Response Distribution ★★★

the pattern or spread of responses selected by test-takers for each option in a test item; used to analyze how test-takers are responding and evaluate item quality

⑦ Distractor 기출 ★★

any of the incorrect options in a multiple-choice item

⑧ Constructed-response Item ★★★

a type of test item or test task that requires test takers to respond to series of open-ended questions by writing, speaking, or doing something rather than choose answers from a ready-made list. The most commonly used types of constructed-response items include fill-in, short-answer, and performance assessment.

STEP 03 **Apply the Key Terms in Practice**

1 Principles

Fill in the blanks with the most appropriate terms.

🔷 **Teacher 1**

I designed a speaking test for my first-year high school students, and I focused on making sure the tasks reflected what we covered in class. Since the topics were directly based on the textbook and in-class discussions, I believe the test had strong ⓐ _____. I also created role-play tasks like ordering food at a restaurant or asking for directions to make the tasks resemble real-life communication. This helped increase the test's ⓑ _____ and made students feel the assessment was meaningful.

🔷 **Teacher 2**

Two teachers, including myself, scored the recent writing test using the same rubric. Before grading, we discussed the criteria and practiced with sample essays to minimize scoring differences. As a result, I believe the test achieved high ⓒ _____. In addition, I checked that the rubric categories were well aligned and consistently measured the intended writing construct. This suggests the test demonstrated strong ⓓ _____ across different sections.

🔷 **Teacher 3**

For my speaking assessment, I wanted to balance accuracy with efficiency. To ensure ⓔ _____, I limited each student's test time to four minutes and kept the number of tasks manageable. On test day, I arranged the classroom carefully so there were no distractions, technical issues, or background noise, ensuring the test environment was stable and fair. I believe these steps improved the overall ⓕ _____ of the assessment.

🔶 Teacher 4

After reviewing my listening test, I realized some tasks only measured students' ability to match keywords rather than their overall listening comprehension. This made me question the test's ⑨ _____, since it didn't fully capture the broader construct I wanted to assess. To improve, I revised the tasks to measure students' ability to interpret meaning and infer speakers' intentions. Afterward, students reported that they started focusing more on listening strategies in class, which shows the test produced a positive ⓗ _____ effect on their learning.

🔶 Teacher 5

I created a speaking test for my advanced students, and I wanted it to appear appropriate and relevant so they would feel confident that it measured what it claimed to measure. I believe the tasks had strong ⓘ _____ because students said the scenarios looked realistic and connected to the course objectives. After the test, I compared the students' scores with their future oral presentation performance to evaluate the test's ⓙ _____. I also checked their results against a validated speaking exam, confirming good alignment and thus supporting the test's ⓚ _____.

🔶 Teacher 6

For my recent essay-writing test, I graded all the papers twice–once immediately after the test and once a few days later–to ensure my own scoring was consistent. Because I gave nearly the same scores both times, I believe the test showed strong ⓛ _____. Additionally, to increase fairness, I compared my scores with those of another teacher using the same rubric. After a calibration session, our scoring differences were minimal, which demonstrates solid ⓒ _____ as well.

❷ Types of Assessment

Read the comments below and fill in the blanks by identifying the type of test that each teacher applied.

⬡ Ms. Yoo – ⓐ _____ Testing

> Ms. Yoo designs a grammar-focused midterm exam. Each question tests one isolated language point, such as ：
>
> • *Choose the correct verb form*： *"She* _ _ _ _ _ *(go) to school every day."*
> • *Fill in the blank with the correct preposition*： *"He is good* _ _ _ _ _ *math."*
>
> The test includes 40 multiple-choice and fill-in-the-blank items. Since each item measures a single, independent skill, students can still perform well even if they do not fully understand the entire passage or context.

⬡ Ms. Park – ⓑ _____ Testing

> Ms. Park creates a dictation test for the midterm exam. Students listen to a short passage twice and complete the dictation task by filling in 10 missing words or short phrases. This task requires students to combine multiple language skills. They need to use their listening skills to understand the overall passage and locate the missing information, as well as their grammar and vocabulary knowledge to choose the correct forms and words for each blank. In addition, they use reading comprehension to review the completed passage and ensure that it makes sense.

❸ Cloze Test

Read the conversation between two teachers and fill in the blanks with the most appropriate terms.

Ms. Lee : I'm planning to use a cloze test for my students, but I'm not sure which type to choose.

Mr. Choi : Let's start with the ⓐ _____ cloze test. That's where you delete every nth word, like every 5th or 7th. It's simple to make, but sometimes unimportant words get deleted.

Ms. Lee : Right. That's why the ⓑ _____ type is useful. Instead of deleting words mechanically, we choose specific target words based on our goals, like connectors or key vocabulary.

Mr. Choi : So ⓐ _____ is easier, but ⓑ _____ is more focused. But both only check missing words, right?

Ms. Lee : Exactly. That's why I'm considering the ⓒ _____. It deletes the second half of every second word, so students get a clue from the first part. It's slightly easier but still tests overall proficiency well.

Mr. Choi : Got it. And if we want to test students' discourse-level comprehension, we could try a(n) ⓓ _____ test.

Ms. Lee : Yes. In a(n) ⓓ _____ test, whole phrases or sentences are missing, and students rebuild meaning from the context. It's good for checking higher-level understanding.

Mr. Choi : That makes sense. Each type complements the others. Maybe combining them would give a more balanced assessment.

Ms. Lee : I agree. I might use ⓑ _____ for vocabulary and connectors, but add a short ⓓ _____ task to test overall comprehension.

4 Classroom Testing Types

Read the four teachers' comments and fill in the blanks with the appropriate test types.

⬡ Teacher 1 – ⓐ _____ Test

Some of my students are preparing for English camps and exchange programs abroad. I want to check their **overall English ability**, not just what we've covered in class. I need a test that measures their **general language competence** so I can recommend suitable programs for them. It doesn't have to match my class content– it just needs to reflect their true proficiency.

⬡ Teacher 2 – ⓑ _____ Test

Next semester, I'll have a new group of students from different classes, and their **proficiency levels are very mixed**. Before the semester begins, I want to **place them into appropriate groups** based on their current abilities. I need a test that sorts students into levels rather than measuring what they've learned so far.

⬡ Teacher 3 – ⓒ _____ Test

I'm planning a new writing unit, but before starting, I want to **find out my students' strengths and weaknesses**. Some may already understand sentence structure, while others might struggle with vocabulary or organization. I need a test that identifies these **specific problem areas before instruction begins**, so I can design lessons that better match their needs.

⬡ Teacher 4 – ⓓ _____ Test

I just finished a **12-week speaking project**, and now I want to measure **how much my students have learned**. I need a test that is **closely linked to the course objectives** so I can see how well they understood what we covered. I'm less interested in their overall proficiency–I just want to know their **progress based on what was taught**.

---

⑤ Alternative Assessment

Read the three students' reviews and fill in the blanks with the most appropriate terms.

🔷 Soyeon

"This semester, our teacher asked us to create a(n) ⓐ _____ of our writing tasks. I collected my drafts, final essays, and reflection notes for each assignment. At first, it felt like extra work, but as I reviewed my earlier pieces, I could see **how much my writing had improved** over time. Organizing everything made me realize which grammar mistakes I kept repeating and which areas I had mastered. I liked that the portfolio showed **my overall progress**, not just one test score. It made me feel proud of what I achieved."

🔷 Jihun

"Today, we did a(n) ⓑ _____ after our speaking activity. The teacher gave us a checklist with categories like fluency, pronunciation, and use of expressions. I listened to the recording of my presentation and scored myself. At first, it was uncomfortable to evaluate my own mistakes, but it helped me **notice patterns** in my speaking, like how often I paused or used filler words. I realized I need to work on organizing my ideas better. I felt more **responsible for my own learning** because I wasn't just waiting for the teacher's score."

🔷 Minji

"In today's class, we tried ⓒ _____ after the group debate. We exchanged feedback forms and rated our partner's performance based on clarity, evidence, and interaction. At first, I worried about giving low scores to my friends, but the teacher reminded us to **focus on constructive comments** instead of judging. Listening carefully to my partner's arguments helped me learn **new expressions** and strategies for my own speaking. I also realized that **giving feedback** can improve my skills as much as receiving it."

Chapter 08

6 Testing Purpose

Read the two teaching logs and fill in the blanks with the most appropriate terms.

🔖 **Ms. Yoo's Teaching Log**

Today, I conducted a(n) ⓐ _____ assessment to evaluate my students' overall achievement at the end of the speaking unit. The test included three short tasks, and I graded them based on my own judgment of fluency and coherence.

After scoring, I analyzed the results using a(n) ⓑ _____ approach to compare students' performance with the rest of the class. My goal was to identify top-performing students and show everyone where they stood in relation to their peers. I thought this would motivate them to improve.

🔖 **Jihyeon's Learning Log**

Honestly, I felt frustrated after today's speaking test. Since it was a(n) ⓐ _____ assessment, I only had one chance to show my ability, and there weren't enough opportunities to practice or get feedback beforehand. I wish we had more ⓒ _____ assessment during the unit so I could improve step by step before completing the course work.

Another problem was that I only received my rank compared to my classmates. I wanted to know whether I actually met the specific criteria for fluency, vocabulary, and organization. If Ms. Yoo had used a(n) ⓓ _____ assessment with clear performance standards, I would have understood what I did well and what I need to improve. Just knowing my position in the class wasn't helpful for my learning.

---

7 Scoring Student Writing

Read the data below and fill in the blanks with the most appropriate terms.

Korean 1st-grade middle school students complete a writing task expressing their opinion on school uniforms. The teacher uses different scoring approaches depending on the instructional purposes and assessment goal.

ⓐ _____

To quickly screen students' overall performance, Mr. Kim first uses a holistic rubric with 5 performance bands (1-5), each describing overall writing quality. He reads each paragraph and assigns a score based on his general impression of coherence, organization, and language use, matching it to the closest descriptor.

→ ⓐ _____ is efficient and appropriate for large classes or low-stakes assessments, but offer limited feedback for learners.

ⓑ _____

For more detailed classroom feedback, Mr. Kim later switches to ⓑ _____, using a rubric with separate categories: content, organization, grammar, vocabulary, mechanics. Each component is scored separately on 0-5 scale. This allows students to see which specific areas they need to improve.

→ ⓑ _____ provides greater washback for instruction by pinpointing learner strengths and weaknesses.

ⓒ _____

In another class, Mr. Kim uses a(n) ⓒ _____ approach for a more focused task: "Write an email requesting information." Here, he scores students only on how effectively they make the request, because the communicative function (requesting) is the main goal of the task.

→ ⓒ _____ is ideal for purpose-driven tasks, where one communicative function is prioritized above all else.

8 Testing Items

Read the conversation between two teachers and fill in the blanks with the most appropriate terms.

Ms. Yoo : I've been using only ⓐ _____ items for my reading assessments. They're easy to grade and give reliable scores because there's only one correct answer. But I feel like I'm not getting the full picture of my students' abilities.

Ms. Park : I understand. That type of item is efficient, but it mostly measure recognition rather than production. Sometimes students choose the right answer without fully understanding the passage.

Ms. Yoo : Exactly! That's what I've noticed. Some students get high scores, but when I ask them to explain, they can't summarize the passage or justify their answers.

Ms. Park : In that case, you might want to include ⓑ _____ items. These ask students to write their own answers, like summarizing the author's opinion or explaining the reasoning behind their choice. It helps you measure critical thinking and expressive skills.

Ms. Yoo : That makes sense, but grading would take so much longer, especially with large classes.

Ms. Park : True, but you can prepare a clear rubric to make scoring more consistent and fair. Or, you could combine both types–use multiple-choice for checking specific facts or vocabulary and add one or two constructed-response questions to assess deeper understanding.

Ms. Yoo : I like that idea. A mixed assessment would be more valid and give me a better picture of my students' reading skills. I'll redesign my test to balance efficiency and depth.

⑨ Multiple Choice Testing

Read the data below and follow the directions.

> *Below is a(n)* ⓐ _____ *table, which shows how many students in the high-performing group and low-performing group selected each option for each test item.*
>
> 🔷 ⓐ _____
>
> Number of students : 30
>
> | | | A | B | C | D |
> |---|---|---|---|---|---|
> | Item 1 | High-ability students (n=15) | 1 | 14* | 0 | 0 |
> | | Low-ability students (n=15) | 1 | 12* | 1 | 1 |
> | Item 2 | High-ability students (n=15) | 6 | 3 | 5* | 1 |
> | | Low-ability students (n=15) | 1 | 1 | 12* | 1 |
> | Item 3 | High-ability students (n=15) | 2 | 1 | 0 | 12* |
> | | Low-ability students (n=15) | 7 | 2 | 0 | 6* |
>
> * is the answer.

Referring to the data above, fill in the blanks with the most appropriate terms.

The ⓐ _____ analysis revealed several key insights into the test items. The ⓑ _____, which is calculated as the proportion of students who answered the item correctly, was .87 for Item 1, showing that the item was too easy and therefore has limited usefulness for measuring student ability. However, ⓒ _____ analysis indicated a concern with Item 2, which showed ⓓ _____ as more low-performing students answered correctly than high-performing students, reducing its validity. In terms of ⓔ _____, Item 3 contained an ineffective distractor since Option C was never selected, while Item 2 had a misleading distractor that confused many high scorers.

Answers

1 Principles

ⓐ content validity

ⓑ authenticity

ⓒ inter-rater reliability

ⓓ internal consistency

ⓔ practicality

ⓕ administration reliability

ⓖ construct validity

ⓗ washback

ⓘ face validity

ⓙ predictive validity

ⓚ concurrent validity

ⓛ intra-rater reliability

2 Types of Assessment

ⓐ Discrete-point

ⓑ Integrative

3 Cloze Test

ⓐ fixed-ratio deletion

ⓑ rational deletion

ⓒ C-test

ⓓ reconstruction

4 Classroom Testing Types

ⓐ Proficiency

ⓑ Placement

ⓒ Diagnostic

ⓓ Achievement

5 Alternative Assessment

ⓐ portfolio

ⓑ self-assessment

ⓒ peer-assessment

6 Testing Purpose

ⓐ summative

ⓑ norm-referenced

ⓒ formative

ⓓ criterion-referenced

7 Scoring Student Writing

ⓐ Holistic Scoring

ⓑ Analytic Scoring / analytic scoring

ⓒ Primary Trait Scoring / primary trait scoring

8 Testing Items

ⓐ multiple-choice

ⓑ constructed-response

9 Multiple Choice Testing

ⓐ response frequency distribution / Response Frequency Distribution

ⓑ item facility

ⓒ item discrimination

ⓓ negative discrimination

ⓔ distractor analysis

Chapter 08

Index

Index

초판인쇄 | 2025. 11. 3. **초판발행** | 2025. 11. 7.

공저자 | 박현수·유다현 **발행인** | 박 용

발행처 | (주)박문각출판 **표지디자인** | 박문각 디자인팀

등록 | 2015년 4월 29일 제2019-000137호

주소 | 06654 서울시 서초구 효령로 283 서경B/D 4층

팩스 | (02)584-2927

전화 | 교재 주문·내용 문의 (02)6466-7202

정가 17,000원   ISBN 979-11-7519-319-2